First published in 2019 by
Clarity Media Ltd
www.clarity-media.co.uk

Content by Conor Byrne
Design and Layout by Lauren Spurgeon

About Clarity Media

Clarity Media are a leading provider of a huge range of puzzles for adults and children. For more information on our services, please visit us at www.pzle.co.uk. For information on purchasing puzzles for publication, visit us at www.clarity-media.co.uk

Puzzle Magazines

If you enjoy the puzzles in this book, then you may be interested in our puzzle magazines. We have a very large range of magazines that you can download and print yourself in PDF format at our Puzzle Magazine site. For more information, take a look at www.puzzle-magazine.com

Online Puzzles

If you prefer to play puzzles online, please take a look at the Puzzle Club website, at www.thepuzzleclub.com

**We also have more puzzle books available at
www.puzzle-book.co.uk**

...Contents...

...Instructions...

Welcome to this fantastic collection of 100 brand new crosswords with a history themed clue to help you solve each puzzle. In addition to the usual crossword, the puzzles in this book have a fun bonus twist: hidden in the shaded squares in each grid is a history-themed word. A clue to the word is given at the top of each puzzle, and the entry grid at the bottom of each puzzle helps you unscramble the letters to find the theme word.

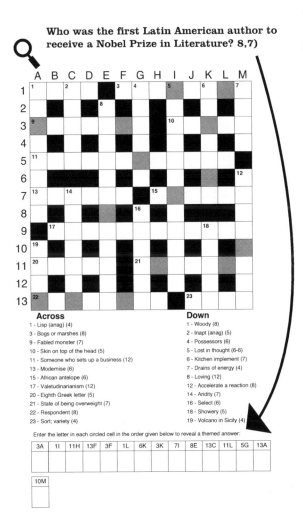

Who was the first Latin American author to receive a Nobel Prize in Literature? 8,7)

Across
1 - Lisp (anag) (4)
3 - Bogs or marshes (8)
9 - Fabled monster (7)
10 - Skin on top of the head (5)
11 - Someone who sets up a business (12)
13 - Modernise (6)
15 - African antelope (6)
17 - Valetudinarianism (12)
20 - Eighth Greek letter (5)
21 - State of being overweight (7)
22 - Respondent (8)
23 - Sort; variety (4)

Down
1 - Woody (8)
2 - Inapt (anag) (5)
4 - Possessors (6)
5 - Lost in thought (6-6)
6 - Kitchen implement (7)
7 - Drains of energy (4)
8 - Loving (12)
12 - Accelerate a reaction (8)
14 - Aridity (7)
16 - Select (6)
18 - Showery (5)
19 - Volcano in Sicily (4)

Enter the letter in each circled cell in the order given below to reveal a themed answer:

3A	1I	11H	13F	3F	1L	6K	3K	7I	8E	13C	11L	5G	13A

10M

You can use the themed word whenever you wish to get more hints about the grid. If you can solve the clue straightaway and write in the themed word, then you will reveal several more letters in the grid to help you make progress solving the crossword. Or you can note down the letters in the shaded squares as you go along and solve both elements of the puzzle at the same time.

We hope you enjoy these fun, themed, crossword puzzles!

Clue: How many British colonies were founded on the Atlantic coast of North America during the seventeenth- and eighteenth-centuries? (8)

Across

1 - People who fly airplanes (6)
7 - Negotiator (8)
8 - Not me (3)
9 - Capital of Ireland (6)
10 - Regretted (4)
11 - Unit of capacitance (5)
13 - Very foolish (7)
15 - Fish with sharp teeth (7)
17 - African mammal (5)
21 - Affirm with confidence (4)
22 - Open a present (6)
23 - Ovoid foodstuff (3)
24 - Draws quickly (8)
25 - Gossip (6)

Down

1 - Profit; reward (6)
2 - Less quiet (6)
3 - Refine metal (5)
4 - Eccentricity (7)
5 - Written guarantee (8)
6 - Mirthless (6)
12 - Sprightliness (8)
14 - Mental process or idea (7)
16 - Call on (6)
18 - Anticipate (6)
19 - Point in an orbit furthest from earth (6)
20 - Distort (5)

Enter the letter in each circled cell in the order given below to reveal a themed answer:

13K	12F	4G	3J	13J	2G	10C	10G

Clue: New York used to be called what? (3,9)

Across

1 - Group of actors in a show (4)
3 - Unauthorized writing on walls (8)
9 - Caring for (7)
10 - Kick out (5)
11 - Awkward (12)
14 - Primary color (3)
16 - Staple food (5)
17 - First woman (3)
18 - Defenseless targets (7,5)
21 - Meat and vegetables on a skewer (5)
22 - Canvas shelters (7)
23 - Feigns (8)
24 - Colors (4)

Down

1 - Capital of Australia (8)
2 - Woody plant (5)
4 - Floor cover (3)
5 - Independent (12)
6 - Encroach (7)
7 - Indolently (4)
8 - Discreditable (12)
12 - Crime of setting something on fire (5)
13 - Population counts (8)
15 - Fall slowly (of a liquid) (7)
19 - Confection made with sugar (5)
20 - Bypass (4)
22 - Sum up (3)

Enter the letter in each circled cell in the order given below to reveal a themed answer:

11I	7K	11H	10E	5B	13H	7H	11B	2I	12G	1B	2K

3

Clue: Who was the last US President from the Whig Party? (7,8)

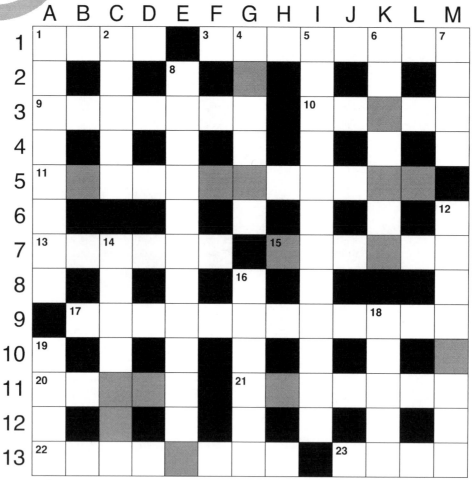

Across

1 - Lowest adult male singing voice (4)
3 - Is composed of (8)
9 - Break; interruption (7)
10 - Cuban dance (5)
11 - From this time (12)
13 - Christening (6)
15 - Breed of sheep (6)
17 - Bump (12)
20 - Head up (5)
21 - Rid of something unpleasant (7)
22 - Uneasy (8)
23 - Reasons; explanations (4)

Down

1 - Tennis stroke (8)
2 - Harsh and serious (5)
4 - Speaker (6)
5 - Sweet red fruits (12)
6 - Japanese warriors (7)
7 - Large bodies of water (4)
8 - Occult (12)
12 - Certain to fail (8)
14 - Human beings (7)
16 - Calculating machine (6)
18 - One divided by nine (5)
19 - Skin mark (4)

Enter the letter in each circled cell in the order given below to reveal a themed answer:

7H	7K	13E	12C	11C	2G	5L	5F	11D	11H	10M	3K	5G	5K

5B

4

Clue: Passed in 1865, which amendment to the United States Constitution abolished slavery? (10)

Across

1 - Cries (4)
3 - Glue (8)
9 - Inclination (7)
10 - Factual evidence (5)
11 - At or to a great height (5)
12 - Small dog (7)
13 - Boil gently (6)
15 - Group of sports teams that play each other (6)
17 - Repeats from memory (7)
18 - Subject (5)
20 - Ingenuous (5)
21 - Become husky (7)
22 - Ultimate (8)
23 - Spur on (4)

Down

1 - Confidence in one's abilities (4-9)
2 - Shout of approval (5)
4 - Fingers (6)
5 - Expel inertia (anag) (12)
6 - Smoothing clothes (7)
7 - Fizz (13)
8 - Abuse (12)
14 - Apparatus (7)
16 - Respiratory condition (6)
19 - Baffling question (5)

Enter the letter in each circled cell in the order given below to reveal a themed answer:

5E	11G	10I	5I	10G	1I	13C	11M	9I	1H

Clue: The 1776 Declaration of Independence was signed and adopted in which city? (12)

Across

1 - Decomposes (6)
7 - Groups of similar things (8)
8 - Common illness (abbrev.) (3)
9 - Ploy (6)
10 - Rank (4)
11 - Abominable snowmen (5)
13 - Visually appealing (7)
15 - Creator (anag) (7)
17 - Small spot (5)
21 - Fencing sword (4)
22 - Document granting invention rights (6)
23 - Sprinted (3)
24 - Midwestern state (8)
25 - Nearer (6)

Down

1 - Dexterously (6)
2 - Trapped (6)
3 - Underwater breathing device (5)
4 - Window furnishing (7)
5 - Spacecraft (8)
6 - Savage (6)
12 - Become greater in size (8)
14 - Self-important (7)
16 - Liveliness (6)
18 - Background actors (6)
19 - Danish monetary unit (pl.) (6)
20 - Seemingly indifferent to emotions (5)

Enter the letter in each circled cell in the order given below to reveal a themed answer:

7F	6J	6H	13I	11D	1A	13D	2G	8J	5C	12H	2C

6

Clue: What is the term for the group of liberal arts colleges in the Northeastern United States founded between 1837 and 1889? (5,7)

Across

1 - Meat from a calf (4)
3 - Eg London and Paris (8)
9 - Return to poor health (7)
10 - Erect (3,2)
11 - Scientific research rooms (12)
14 - Golf peg (3)
16 - Funny person (5)
17 - Lyric poem (3)
18 - Non-governmental fighting force (12)
21 - Island in the Bay of Naples (5)
22 - Eg relating to touch or taste (7)
23 - Face-to-face conversation (3-2-3)
24 - Give temporarily (4)

Down

1 - Masculinity (8)
2 - Speak without preparation (2-3)
4 - Excellent tennis serve (3)
5 - Directions (12)
6 - Decorative style of the 1920s and 1930s (3,4)
7 - Drains of energy (4)
8 - Gratitude (12)
12 - Musical times (5)
13 - Naively innocent (4-4)
15 - Something showing a general rule (7)
19 - Make right (5)
20 - Reflect sound (4)
22 - Violate a law of God (3)

Enter the letter in each circled cell in the order given below to reveal a themed answer:

4M	3G	1A	6G	13B	11J	6A	5L	4I	5K	11D	3I

Clue: Which treaty, signed on 3 September 1783, ended the American Revolutionary War? (5)

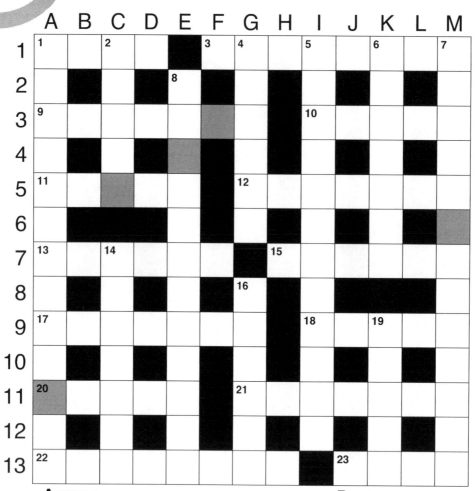

Across

1 - Snug (4)
3 - Submissive to authority (8)
9 - Heist (7)
10 - The papal court (5)
11 - Shaped like an egg (5)
12 - Tidies (7)
13 - Elaborately decorated (6)
15 - Frequently repeated phrase (6)
17 - Severely simple (7)
18 - Accustom (5)
20 - Suffuse with color (5)
21 - Lock of curly hair (7)
22 - Opposite of positive (8)
23 - Remain (4)

Down

1 - Confirmation (13)
2 - Striped animal (5)
4 - To or until a later time (6)
5 - Formal announcements (12)
6 - Serious (7)
7 - Party lanterns (anag) (13)
8 - Transportation of people to a new area (12)
14 - Horse feeder (7)
16 - History play by Shakespeare (5,1)
19 - Not illuminated (5)

Enter the letter in each circled cell in the order given below to reveal a themed answer:

6M	5C	3F	11A	4E

8

Clue: Which era of social activism and political reform spanned from the 1890s to the 1920s? (11)

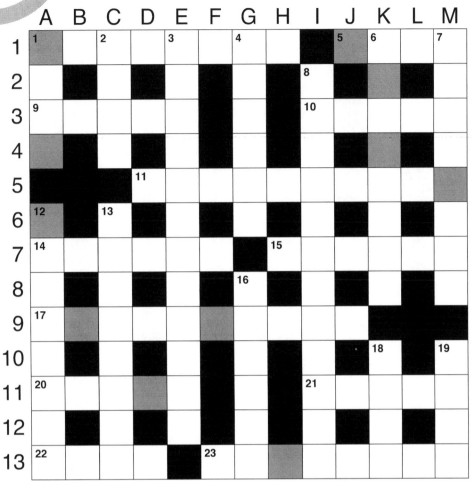

Across

1 - Hitting repeatedly (8)
5 - Block a decision (4)
9 - Broaden (5)
10 - Undo; loosen (5)
11 - Merge into one structure (10)
14 - Voice box (6)
15 - Mix with (6)
17 - Fellow national (10)
20 - Relating to sound (5)
21 - Adult insect (5)
22 - Current (4)
23 - Distinct personality of an individual (8)

Down

1 - Animal feet (4)
2 - Official language of Pakistan (4)
3 - Name; designation (12)
4 - Head; noggin (6)
6 - Alienate (8)
7 - Fully aware (4-4)
8 - Philanthropic (12)
12 - Cover with ice or snow (8)
13 - Focused and level-headed (8)
16 - Large indefinite number (6)
18 - The wise men (4)
19 - Squarish in shape (4)

Enter the letter in each circled cell in the order given below to reveal a themed answer:

1A	9F	9B	6A	4K	13H	4A	2K	11D	1J	5M

Clue: Which 1927 film won the first Academy Award for Best Picture? (5)

Across

1 - Opposite of an acid (6)
7 - Physical weakness (8)
8 - Longing (3)
9 - Questions intensely (6)
10 - Radar echo (4)
11 - Injure (5)
13 - Company that supplies food (7)
15 - Henry David ___ : US author and poet (7)
17 - Sorts (5)
21 - Ballet skirt (4)
22 - Plants of the agave family (6)
23 - Turn upside down (3)
24 - Small North American avian (8)
25 - Governor in ancient Persia (6)

Down

1 - In a careless manner (6)
2 - Martial art (4,2)
3 - Effigies (5)
4 - At the ocean floor (7)
5 - Swollen with fat (8)
6 - Hit (6)
12 - Brought up; cared for (8)
14 - Care for children (7)
16 - Occurring every sixty minutes (6)
18 - Large printed notice (6)
19 - Mistake (4-2)
20 - Moves swiftly (5)

Enter the letter in each circled cell in the order given below to reveal a themed answer:

6A	11L	2A	4C	8M

Clue: Which nationwide railroad strike lasted from 11 May to 20 July 1894? (7,6)

Across

1 - Quickness of perception (6)
5 - Continue after a break (6)
8 - Char (4)
9 - Lack of color (8)
10 - Grim (5)
11 - Torment or harass (7)
14 - Economical (4-9)
16 - As a whole (2,5)
18 - Facial expression (5)
20 - Spine (8)
22 - Center of rotation (4)
23 - Recognition (6)
24 - Sharp pain (6)

Down

2 - Lead-up to a rocket launch (9)
3 - Tall slender tower (7)
4 - Bites sharply (4)
5 - Reassured (8)
6 - Eg taste or touch (5)
7 - Form of address for a married woman (3)
12 - Including (9)
13 - Subsidiary (8)
15 - Very large drums (7)
17 - Made a request (5)
19 - US monetary unit (4)
21 - Mixture of gases we breathe (3)

Enter the letter in each circled cell in the order given below to reveal a themed answer:

3F	1K	9L	3H	1L	9D	12H	3L	7D	3C	7K	11D	1I

11

Clue: The Beaver Wars of 1629-1701 were fought between the Algonquians and which Native American group? (8)

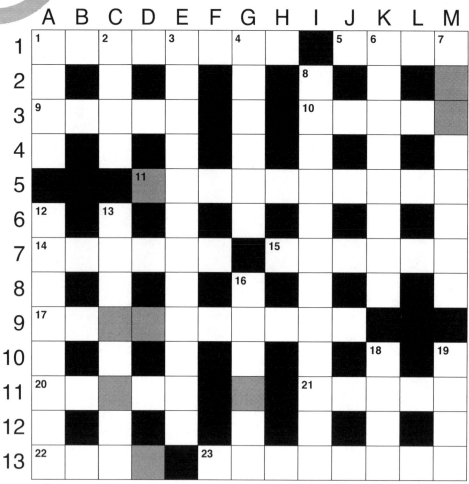

Across

1 - Able to be easily carried (8)
5 - Sour-tasting substance (4)
9 - Very silly or affected (5)
10 - Tests (5)
11 - Container (10)
14 - Connected (6)
15 - Short pieces of writing (6)
17 - Consecutive (10)
20 - Authoritative proclamation (5)
21 - Expel from a country (5)
22 - Small toy (2-2)
23 - Excited or annoyed (8)

Down

1 - Take part in a sport (4)
2 - Liquid precipitation (4)
3 - Accomplishments (12)
4 - Marine gastropod mollusk (6)
6 - Form of carbon (8)
7 - Distribute (8)
8 - Part of the Bible (3,9)
12 - Gusty (8)
13 - Unfairness (8)
16 - Powerful; tough (6)
18 - Baseball glove (4)
19 - Nuisance plant (4)

Enter the letter in each circled cell in the order given below to reveal a themed answer:

11C	5D	11G	9C	9D	13D	2M	3M

12

Clue: What was the surname of the 10th US President? (5)

	A	B	C	D	E	F	G	H	I	J	K	L	M
1	1		2			3	4		5		6		7
2					8								
3	9								10				
4													
5	11												
6													12
7	13		14						15				
8							16						
9		17									18		
10	19												
11	20						21						
12													
13	22								23				

Across

1 - Part of twilight (4)
3 - Not genuine (8)
9 - Part of an orchestra (7)
10 - Destitute (5)
11 - In the order of the letters from A to Z (12)
13 - Fast-flowing part of a river (6)
15 - German astronomer (6)
17 - Aversion to change (12)
20 - Lessen (5)
21 - Copious (7)
22 - Apparition (8)
23 - Musical instrument (4)

Down

1 - Gives up any hope (8)
2 - Throw away (5)
4 - Elapsed (of time) (6)
5 - Significantly (12)
6 - Generally (7)
7 - States (4)
8 - Radiant (12)
12 - First public performance (8)
14 - Proportionately (3,4)
16 - Moves slowly and aimlessly (6)
18 - Creamy-white substance (5)
19 - Produce a grating sound (4)

Enter the letter in each circled cell in the order given below to reveal a themed answer:

12G	3M	5B	13M	12M

Clue: In 1969, who became the first person to walk on the Moon? (4,9)

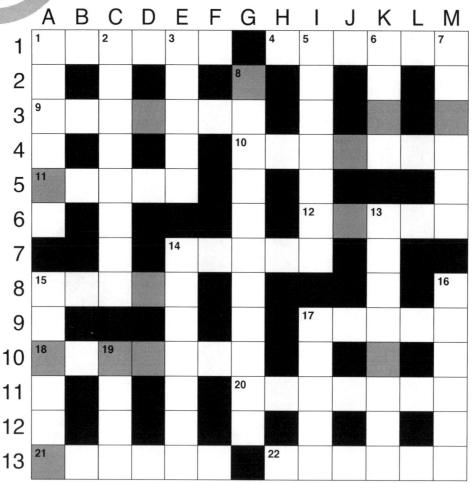

Across

1 - Flowers (6)
4 - Lessens (6)
9 - A parent's mother (7)
10 - Element with atomic number 31 (7)
11 - Clamorous (5)
12 - Dish of raw vegetables (5)
14 - Trench (5)
15 - Swiftness or speed (5)
17 - Religious book (5)
18 - Art of paper-folding (7)
20 - Eg from Juneau (7)
21 - Explanation (6)
22 - Not written in any key (of music) (6)

Down

1 - Starts (6)
2 - Musical wind instruments (8)
3 - Dirty (5)
5 - Expecting a rise in stock prices (7)
6 - ___ Amos: US singer-songwriter (4)
7 - Appeared to be (6)
8 - Dictatorial (11)
13 - Type of leather (8)
14 - In reality; actually (2,5)
15 - Herbert ___ : 31st US President (6)
16 - Occurring in spring (6)
17 - Brag (5)
19 - Black ___ : bird found in Colombia (4)

Enter the letter in each circled cell in the order given below to reveal a themed answer:

5A	3M	10C	4J	6J	13A	2G	10K	8D	3K	10A	3D	10D

14

Clue: Announced in 1947, which foreign policy sought to counter Soviet geopolitical expansion during the Cold War? (6,8)

Across
1 - Official population count (6)
5 - Relating to a leg bone (6)
8 - Entry document (4)
9 - Not closed (of an envelope) (8)
10 - Short musical composition (5)
11 - Money owed that cannot be recovered (3,4)
14 - Unbelievable (13)
16 - Ways of doing things (7)
18 - Implant (5)
20 - Beneficial (8)
22 - Release (4)
23 - Selected (6)
24 - Dreary (6)

Down
2 - Being (9)
3 - Unnamed person or thing (2-3-2)
4 - Keep away from (4)
5 - State in Australia (8)
6 - Committee (5)
7 - Consumed food (3)
12 - Female dancer (9)
13 - Corrosive precipitation (4,4)
15 - Having no purpose (7)
17 - Periods of 60 minutes (5)
19 - Pair (4)
21 - Powdery residue (3)

Enter the letter in each circled cell in the order given below to reveal a themed answer:

5B	4J	11D	9J	13L	3G	9M	2J	7F	1H	12D	11L	12L	11J

15

Clue: Which American Civil War battle took place between 30 April and 6 May 1863? (16)

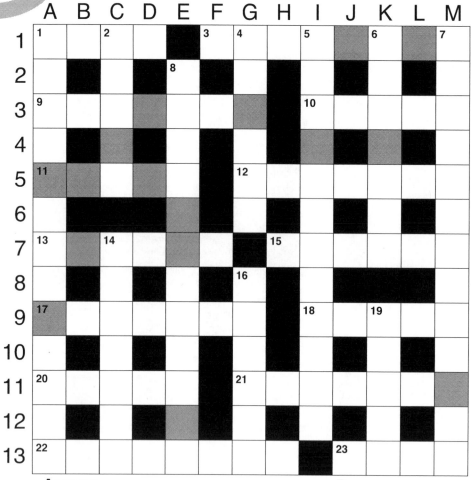

Across

- 1 - Ashen (4)
- 3 - Slipcase (anag) (8)
- 9 - Opposite of later (7)
- 10 - Go over again (5)
- 11 - Make law (5)
- 12 - Messenger (7)
- 13 - Topics for debate (6)
- 15 - State confidently (6)
- 17 - Military aviation facility (3,4)
- 18 - Automaton (5)
- 20 - Maladroit (5)
- 21 - Import barrier (7)
- 22 - Gibberish (8)
- 23 - Purposes (4)

Down

- 1 - Intent (13)
- 2 - Immature insect (5)
- 4 - Copyright theft (6)
- 5 - Draw a figure around another (12)
- 6 - Repository (7)
- 7 - Believing in the power of magic or luck (13)
- 8 - Gossip (6-6)
- 14 - Operating doctor (7)
- 16 - Attacks on all sides (6)
- 19 - Feathered creatures (5)

Enter the letter in each circled cell in the order given below to reveal a themed answer:

5D	4K	9A	5B	4I	7E	6E	12E	11M	3G	7B	4C	1J	1L	3D	5A

18

16

Clue: What is the term for those who came of age during the First World War? (4,10)

Across

1 - Killer whale (4)
3 - Prompt (8)
9 - Buddies (7)
10 - Be more successful than (5)
11 - Clothing shop (12)
13 - Experience again (6)
15 - Relating to stars (6)
17 - Greedily (12)
20 - One of the United Arab Emirates (5)
21 - Baked pasta dish (7)
22 - Infinite time (8)
23 - Narrow part of something (4)

Down

1 - Situated at sea (8)
2 - Ascend (5)
4 - Cause to fall from a horse (6)
5 - Frame on which to hang garments (12)
6 - Speaker (7)
7 - Apparatus for weaving (4)
8 - Shyness (12)
12 - Reproduce recorded sound (4,4)
14 - Habitable (7)
16 - Wildcat (6)
18 - Smooth transition (5)
19 - Lazy (4)

Enter the letter in each circled cell in the order given below to reveal a themed answer:

2I	3M	3G	7J	11K	4G	1H	7F	10I	11J	4I	13F	1A	2G

17

Clue: Who was the first actor to receive a posthumous Academy Award nomination for Best Actor? (5,4)

Across

1 - Halting (8)
5 - Ridge of rock (4)
8 - Saturate (5)
9 - Outburst of anger (7)
10 - Agrees (7)
12 - The kneading of muscles and joints (7)
14 - Built up (7)
16 - Gave a prize (7)
18 - Annoying (7)
19 - Assess; rank (5)
20 - University in Connecticut (4)
21 - Surname of Judas (8)

Down

1 - Moderately well (2-2)
2 - Musical dramas (6)
3 - Inhabited (9)
4 - See (6)
6 - Reprimand (6)
7 - Starved (8)
11 - Country in Central America (9)
12 - System of conduct and values (8)
13 - Wild dog (6)
14 - Words of farewell (6)
15 - Adventurous expedition (6)
17 - Taylor ___ : US tennis player (4)

Enter the letter in each circled cell in the order given below to reveal a themed answer:

8C	13I	3M	7M	5M	11L	1L	8I	12M

18

Clue: Completed in 1941, Mount Rushmore National Memorial is located in which US state? (5,6)

Across

1 - Impound during a war (6)
4 - Soak up (6)
9 - Avoidance (7)
10 - Deer meat (7)
11 - Finds agreeable (5)
12 - All (5)
14 - Intimate companion (5)
15 - Way or course taken (5)
17 - Be; live (5)
18 - Childbirth assistant (7)
20 - Small Arctic whale (7)
21 - Maxim (6)
22 - Colored parts of eyes; flowers (6)

Down

1 - Standards of perfection (6)
2 - Expression of gratitude (5,3)
3 - Narrow leather strips (5)
5 - Light that flashes on and off (7)
6 - Nocturnal birds (4)
7 - Monetary reward (6)
8 - Participation (11)
13 - Improves in flavor (8)
14 - Vocabulary list (7)
15 - Whispers; pieces of gossip (6)
16 - Plant stems (6)
17 - Mistake (5)
19 - Declare to be untrue (4)

Enter the letter in each circled cell in the order given below to reveal a themed answer:

8M	7C	9A	9M	2C	2A	11L	12M	4L	1C	1H

19

Clue: Who was the 12th President of the United States? (7,6)

Across

1 - Sorriest (anag) (8)
5 - Greek cheese (4)
8 - Pond-dwelling amphibians (5)
9 - Loss of memory (7)
10 - Seriously (7)
12 - Extraordinary occurrence (7)
14 - Surpasses (7)
16 - Stirred (7)
18 - Imaginary (7)
19 - Male duck (5)
20 - Uncertain of one's location (4)
21 - Rush of animals (8)

Down

1 - Circular band (4)
2 - Woodcutter (6)
3 - Doubt about someone's honesty (9)
4 - Juicy citrus fruit (6)
6 - Follows (6)
7 - Examines in detail (8)
11 - Dutch capital (9)
12 - Compassionate (8)
13 - 16 of these in a pound (6)
14 - Strangest (6)
15 - Period of time without electricity (6)
17 - They used to be (4)

Enter the letter in each circled cell in the order given below to reveal a themed answer:

6M	2C	11C	9B	5I	6C	4C	10K	11K	5M	5L	13B	11J

Clue: *Norma Jeane Mortenson was the birth name of which actress born in 1926? (7,6)*

Across

1 - Positive (6)
4 - Line on a map indicating pressure (6)
9 - Contradiction in terms (7)
10 - Compete (7)
11 - Guide at a wedding (5)
12 - Piece of pottery (5)
14 - Fit; sporting contest (5)
15 - Genre (5)
17 - Negatively charged ion (5)
18 - Residence of the Pope (7)
20 - Pilot (7)
21 - Wanders off; drifts (6)
22 - Collection of things (6)

Down

1 - Disconnect from a socket (6)
2 - Anniversary of when you are born (8)
3 - Tree of the birch family (5)
5 - Eg from Madrid (7)
6 - Support or foundation (4)
7 - Attacked at speed (6)
8 - Extraordinary (11)
13 - Confessed to be the case (8)
14 - Liquid metallic element (7)
15 - Cuts off (6)
16 - False (6)
17 - Word of farewell (5)
19 - Rip up (4)

Enter the letter in each circled cell in the order given below to reveal a themed answer:

7E	6K	12A	9K	4A	13E	4L	8K	4H	9J	9E	9G	4K

Clue: Which American Civil War battle witnessed the largest number of casualties of the entire war? (10)

Across

1 - Formulating (8)
5 - Marine or freshwater fish (4)
8 - Opposite of old (5)
9 - Living in water (7)
10 - Chiefly (7)
12 - Succinctly (7)
14 - Gathered together (7)
16 - ___ Portman: actress (7)
18 - Dry red table wine of Italy (7)
19 - Type of chemical bond (5)
20 - Gets with great difficulty (4)
21 - Final teenage year (8)

Down

1 - Yaps (anag) (4)
2 - Graduates of a college (6)
3 - Onset of darkness (9)
4 - Tidily (6)
6 - Warmer (6)
7 - Area at the rear of a house (8)
11 - Little known (9)
12 - Crustacean (8)
13 - Conflict or struggle (6)
14 - Third sign of the zodiac (6)
15 - Caper (6)
17 - Symbol or graphic (4)

Enter the letter in each circled cell in the order given below to reveal a themed answer:

3E	5K	12I	11F	6G	4A	6A	3I	7M	1H

Clue: Which form of evidence, based upon visions and dreams, was admitted into court during the Salem witch trials? (8)

Across

1 - Seed containers (4)
3 - Colored paper thrown at weddings (8)
9 - Block; obstruct (7)
10 - Woodland primula (5)
11 - Regardless of (12)
14 - Automobile (3)
16 - Smells strongly (5)
17 - Large container (3)
18 - Appraisal that is too high (12)
21 - Annoyed (5)
22 - Absolved (7)
23 - Mammal with a spiny coat (8)
24 - ___ Campbell: Canadian actress (4)

Down

1 - Administrative division (8)
2 - Stage setting (5)
4 - Mineral deposit (3)
5 - Principal face of a building (12)
6 - Israeli city (3,4)
7 - Fairies (4)
8 - Short poem for children (7,5)
12 - Seven (anag) (5)
13 - Participant in a meeting (8)
15 - Severely damaged (7)
19 - Passage (5)
20 - Hit hard (4)
22 - Self-esteem (3)

Enter the letter in each circled cell in the order given below to reveal a themed answer:

9G	5F	5D	5H	8M	2I	4K	3K

Clue: Who was the first American woman to be awarded the Nobel Peace Prize? (4,6)

Across

1 - Solemnly renounce (6)
4 - Symbolic (6)
9 - Container for washing (7)
10 - Absence of sound (7)
11 - Water droplets (5)
12 - Aperture in the eye (5)
14 - Rescues (5)
15 - Spiritual sustenance (5)
17 - Give a false notion of (5)
18 - Denoting knowledge based on theoretical deduction (1,6)
20 - Ear bone (7)
21 - Measuring sticks (6)
22 - Hard to digest (6)

Down

1 - Ratio of reflected to incident light (6)
2 - Discard (8)
3 - Assesses performance (5)
5 - One-eyed giant (7)
6 - Part of speech (4)
7 - Breakfast foodstuff (6)
8 - Remark; comment (11)
13 - Translucently clear (8)
14 - Russian tea urn (7)
15 - Scanty (6)
16 - Put right (6)
17 - Make stupid (5)
19 - Small watercourse (4)

Enter the letter in each circled cell in the order given below to reveal a themed answer:

1C	2E	1K	4J	10A	12M	5A	12E	8A	13F

24

Clue: Which American poet and novelist was born on October 27th, 1932? (6,5)

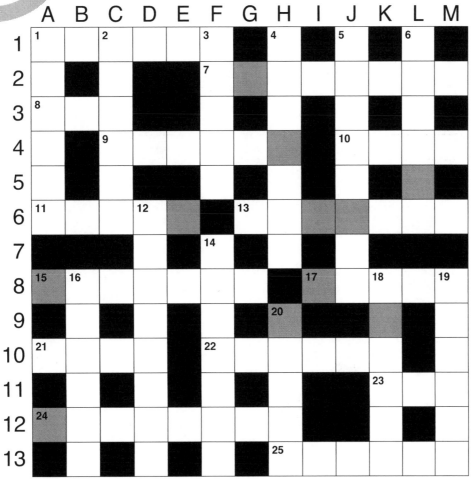

Across

1 - Capital of the Bahamas (6)
7 - ___ Holmes: detective (8)
8 - Sticky substance (3)
9 - Insure (anag) (6)
10 - Loud resonant sound (4)
11 - Bright; cheery (5)
13 - Foolish (7)
15 - Tall stand that supports a book (7)
17 - Equipped with weapons (5)
21 - Opening for air; outlet (4)
22 - Designed for male and female (6)
23 - Anger (3)
24 - Lawyer (8)
25 - Slow pieces of music (6)

Down

1 - Periods of darkness (6)
2 - Relating to monkeys (6)
3 - Supplant (5)
4 - Of enormous effect (7)
5 - Spherical (8)
6 - Exclusive stories (6)
12 - The act of swimming (8)
14 - Squabbling (7)
16 - Happenings (6)
18 - Jumbling up (6)
19 - Puts off (6)
20 - Type of plastic (5)

Enter the letter in each circled cell in the order given below to reveal a themed answer:

4H	6E	8A	9H	9K	8I	5L	6J	12A	6I	2G

Clue: Who was the first person to be appointed US President? (6,10)

Across
- 1 - Cobras (4)
- 3 - Plant with pale yellow flowers (8)
- 9 - Dyestuff (7)
- 10 - Drifter (5)
- 11 - Broadcasting medium (5)
- 12 - Citadel in Moscow (7)
- 13 - Pay no attention to (6)
- 15 - Dwarfed tree (6)
- 17 - Reporter (7)
- 18 - Opposite of true (5)
- 20 - Construct a building (5)
- 21 - Slope (7)
- 22 - Deep ditches (8)
- 23 - Exercise venues (4)

Down
- 1 - Distribution (13)
- 2 - Gaped (anag) (5)
- 4 - Recapture (6)
- 5 - Unemotional and practical (6-2-4)
- 6 - Prophets (7)
- 7 - Ebullience (13)
- 8 - Histrionic (12)
- 14 - Not in any place (7)
- 16 - Ask a person to come (6)
- 19 - People who are not ordained (5)

Enter the letter in each circled cell in the order given below to reveal a themed answer:

13J	5I	4A	11B	7B	9B	9C	4G	13M	13F	5D	11L	3C	12K	8A	7J

26

Clue: What is the term for the competition between the United States and the Soviet Union in spaceflight capability? (5,4)

Across

1 - Unwelcome (8)
5 - Woody plant (4)
8 - Opaque gems (5)
9 - Movement of vehicles en masse (7)
10 - Slanted letters (7)
12 - Exceptionally good (7)
14 - Following (7)
16 - Shorten (7)
18 - Whole number (7)
19 - Slip (5)
20 - Encircle or bind (4)
21 - Dreariness (8)

Down

1 - On top of (4)
2 - Fish with thick lips (6)
3 - Deteriorated rapidly (9)
4 - Necessitate (6)
6 - Fiber for making mats (6)
7 - Letting off (8)
11 - Nervously (9)
12 - Robbing (8)
13 - Author (6)
14 - Intense fear (6)
15 - Stimulate; stir up (6)
17 - Comes together; hair products (4)

Enter the letter in each circled cell in the order given below to reveal a themed answer:

11I	2A	4G	5L	13K	13G	3I	6D	8E

27

Clue: Alice Paul was a leader of which American women's political organization? (8,6,5)

Across

1 - Military conflicts (4)
3 - Enclosure made with posts (8)
9 - Taking a break (7)
10 - Devices for inflating tires (5)
11 - Preliminary (12)
14 - Tear (3)
16 - Be extremely good at (5)
17 - Lay seed in the ground (3)
18 - Having an efficient approach to one's work (12)
21 - Once more (5)
22 - Diminish (7)
23 - Went before (8)
24 - Door by which you leave a building (4)

Down

1 - Soldiers (8)
2 - Steer (anag) (5)
4 - Pull at (3)
5 - Favoring private ownership (12)
6 - Respects (7)
7 - Otherwise (4)
8 - Insubordination (12)
12 - Father's brother (5)
13 - Most saccharine (8)
15 - A bird's feathers collectively (7)
19 - Alphabetical list at the back of a book (5)
20 - Complain unreasonably (4)
22 - Dr ___ : US record producer (3)

Enter the letter in each circled cell in the order given below to reveal a themed answer:

6G	2A	5I	5A	1H	11E	2I	8G	1A	5E	10C	6I	5B	9D

3L	11A	12A	1G	5L

Clue: Which activist has been described as 'First Lady of the Civil Rights Movement'? (7,5,4)

Across

1 - Charge for transportation (4)
3 - Overshadows (8)
9 - Larval salamander (7)
10 - Large musical instrument (5)
11 - Japanese dish (5)
12 - Creepiest (7)
13 - Expend (6)
15 - Soft white fiber (6)
17 - Suggested but not stated explicitly (7)
18 - Wrong (5)
20 - Henrik ___ : Norwegian dramatist (5)
21 - Colored bands of light (7)
22 - Holding close (8)
23 - Buckles (4)

Down

1 - Rotation spins (anag) (13)
2 - Views; observes (5)
4 - Named (6)
5 - Formed a business (12)
6 - Able to pay one's debts (7)
7 - Meteors (8,5)
8 - Inspiring action (12)
14 - Data-entry clerks (7)
16 - Thomas ___ : US inventor (6)
19 - Prologue (abbrev.) (5)

Enter the letter in each circled cell in the order given below to reveal a themed answer:

7H	4M	12M	11D	5M	10A	2G	9L	1G	12A	7J	7C	4C	10G	10K	13H

Clue: Which author wrote the lyrics for 'The Star-Spangled Banner' in 1814? (7,5,3)

Across

1 - Uncover (6)
4 - Drinking vessel (6)
9 - Rise again (7)
10 - Farewell remark (7)
11 - Not telling the truth (5)
12 - Believe in the reliability of (5)
14 - Brief records of information (5)
15 - Dance (5)
17 - Deer (5)
18 - Move (7)
20 - Found (7)
21 - Take small bites out of (6)
22 - Moved back and forth (6)

Down

1 - Disorderly (6)
2 - Spiritually symbolic; esoteric (8)
3 - Show indifference with the shoulders (5)
5 - Exertions (7)
6 - Heavy stick used as a weapon (4)
7 - A mother or father (6)
8 - Unfortunate (11)
13 - Undeserving (8)
14 - Not artificial (7)
15 - Abrupt (6)
16 - Required (6)
17 - Parrot (5)
19 - Wad of absorbent cloth (4)

Enter the letter in each circled cell in the order given below to reveal a themed answer:

3I	3E	10I	8M	6C	5C	1E	8D	1K	4H	6I	4C	1F	3G

4L

Clue: Which siege of 1781 was the last major land battle of the American Revolutionary War? (8)

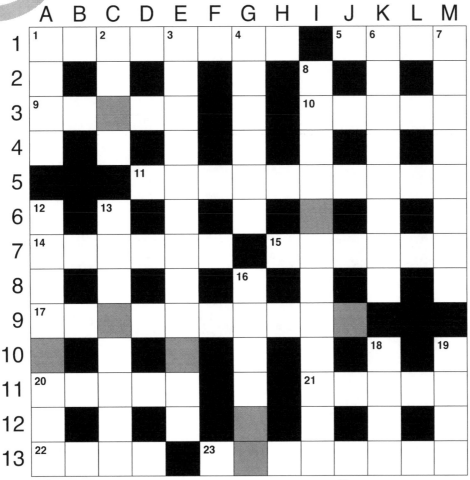

Across

1 - Area of the zodiac (4,4)
5 - Legend (4)
9 - Laud (5)
10 - Domesticated pack animal (5)
11 - Contemptibly (10)
14 - Unexpected; sudden (6)
15 - Conditional release of a prisoner (6)
17 - Formal greeting (3,2,3,2)
20 - Corpulent (5)
21 - Rent (5)
22 - School subject (abbrev.) (4)
23 - Breach of good manners (8)

Down

1 - Grain that grows into a new plant (4)
2 - Opposing (4)
3 - Working for oneself (4-8)
4 - Collections (6)
6 - Annual (8)
7 - Stocky (8)
8 - Badly bruised (5-3-4)
12 - Division of a house (8)
13 - Intimidate with stern words (8)
16 - Gaming tile (6)
18 - Hired form of transport (4)
19 - Wheel that moves a ship's rudder (4)

Enter the letter in each circled cell in the order given below to reveal a themed answer:

10E	9J	10A	6I	3C	13G	9C	12G

31

Clue: Which undertaking during the Second World War produced the first nuclear weapons? (9,7)

Across
1 - Is subject to (6)
4 - Of practical benefit (6)
9 - Base (7)
10 - Break (7)
11 - System of beliefs (5)
12 - Transport by hand (5)
14 - Boorish person (5)
15 - Join together (5)
17 - Card game (5)
18 - Mixed up (7)
20 - Interminable (7)
21 - However; despite that (6)
22 - Slick and shiny (6)

Down
1 - Stupidity (6)
2 - Orchestral pieces with solo instrument (8)
3 - Fanatical (5)
5 - Hot wind blowing from North Africa (7)
6 - Leaf (anag) (4)
7 - Vivacious (6)
8 - Calm and sensible (11)
13 - Careless; rash (8)
14 - Screaming (7)
15 - Not fair (6)
16 - Harsh and unfriendly (6)
17 - Foot-operated lever (5)
19 - Not stereo (4)

Enter the letter in each circled cell in the order given below to reveal a themed answer:

10C	6J	11H	13B	2E	13A	12M	7F	3C	9I	5B	9J	10A	1J

5I	7C

32

Clue: What is Bill Clinton's middle name? (9)

Across

1 - Listen to (4)
3 - Beneficial (8)
9 - Cold-blooded vertebrate like a crocodile (7)
10 - Stove (anag) (5)
11 - Study of microorganisms (12)
14 - Signal for action (3)
16 - Find the answer (5)
17 - Period of time (3)
18 - Physics of movement through air (12)
21 - Additional (5)
22 - Brave (7)
23 - Sprinkling with water (8)
24 - Square measure (4)

Down

1 - Type of book cover (8)
2 - Savory jelly (5)
4 - Cereal grass (3)
5 - Impossible to harm (12)
6 - Tiredness (7)
7 - Get beaten (4)
8 - Designed to distract (12)
12 - Adorn with insertions (5)
13 - Casket (8)
15 - Firearm mechanism (7)
19 - ___ Newton: English physicist (5)
20 - Valuable stones (4)
22 - Enclosed motortruck (3)

Enter the letter in each circled cell in the order given below to reveal a themed answer:

8C	7C	1F	1K	12I	13L	2C	7F	13G

Clue: Who was Barack Obama's Vice President? (3,5)

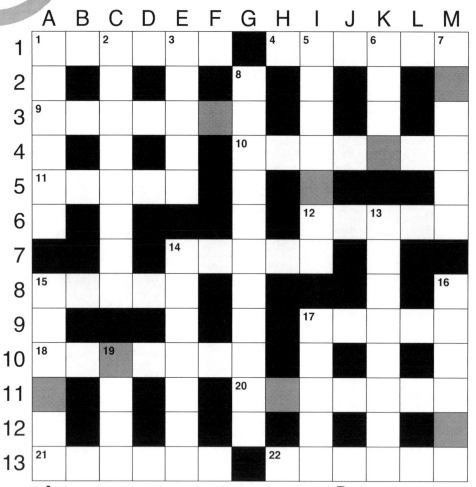

Across

1 - Hate (6)
4 - Unkempt (of hair) (6)
9 - Waterfall (7)
10 - Deserving affection (7)
11 - Standards (5)
12 - Celestial bodies (5)
14 - Disregard rules (5)
15 - Unwarranted (5)
17 - Raise up (5)
18 - Declare to be true (7)
20 - Saves from danger (7)
21 - Delegate a task (6)
22 - Items of value (6)

Down

1 - Shining with light (6)
2 - Of many different kinds (8)
3 - Warms up (5)
5 - The gathering of crops (7)
6 - Insect larva (4)
7 - Songlike cries (6)
8 - Aircraft (pl.) (11)
13 - Innate ability (8)
14 - Giving food to (7)
15 - Country in East Africa (6)
16 - Stagnation or inactivity (6)
17 - Seed cases (5)
19 - Ewers (4)

Enter the letter in each circled cell in the order given below to reveal a themed answer:

10C	2M	11H	4K	12M	3F	5I	11A

Clue: What is the surname of the President from 1901 to 1909? (9)

Across

1 - Religious act (4)
3 - Retort (8)
9 - Insignificant (7)
10 - Golf clubs (5)
11 - Honestly (12)
13 - Tempt (6)
15 - Unfriendly in manner (6)
17 - Unrestrained (12)
20 - Enamel-coated structures in the mouth (5)
21 - River in South America (7)
22 - Catastrophe (8)
23 - Biological unit (4)

Down

1 - Made officially valid (8)
2 - One who always makes an effort (5)
4 - Cream puff (6)
5 - Type of orchestra (12)
6 - Strips of pasta (7)
7 - Relaxation (4)
8 - Garments worn in bed (12)
12 - Group of symptoms which occur together (8)
14 - Large ships (7)
16 - Walked quickly (6)
18 - Set free (5)
19 - Soccer boot grip (4)

Enter the letter in each circled cell in the order given below to reveal a themed answer:

9H	7J	5B	13E	12E	3D	13M	4I	6E

Clue: Which city is the birthplace of the 28th US President, Woodrow Wilson? (8)

Across

1 - Supported (6)
7 - Evoke memories (8)
8 - Young dog (3)
9 - Original (6)
10 - Roll of photographic film (4)
11 - Linear measures of three feet (5)
13 - Rattish (anag) (7)
15 - Scratched (7)
17 - Sacred song (5)
21 - Monetary unit of France (4)
22 - Large shrimp (6)
23 - Excavate (3)
24 - Concise reference work (8)
25 - Well-matched (6)

Down

1 - Subsidiary action (6)
2 - Metallic element (6)
3 - Stage play (5)
4 - Set apart (7)
5 - Robots (8)
6 - Mental or emotional tension (6)
12 - Very hard carbon gems (8)
14 - Fixed sum paid regularly to a person (7)
16 - Puma (6)
18 - Among (6)
19 - Joined together (6)
20 - Shouts orders (5)

Enter the letter in each circled cell in the order given below to reveal a themed answer:

12K	6M	5A	3B	12C	13K	3H	13F

Clue: Which group of women protested in front of the White House for the first time in 1917, for a period of two years? (6,9)

Across

1 - Go ashore (6)
4 - Extreme confusion (6)
9 - Salt lake in the Jordan valley (4,3)
10 - Most tidy (7)
11 - Quotes (5)
12 - Places in position (5)
14 - Perfume (5)
15 - Suit (5)
17 - One who talks wildly (5)
18 - Get too big for something (7)
20 - Made certain of (7)
21 - Inn (6)
22 - Courtroom officials (6)

Down

1 - Work out logically (6)
2 - Launch with great force (of a rocket) (5,3)
3 - Ascends (5)
5 - Wear out completely (7)
6 - Elan (anag) (4)
7 - Maws (6)
8 - Measure of luminous intensity (11)
13 - Journey across (8)
14 - Memory (7)
15 - Decorative ornament (6)
16 - Groups of lions (6)
17 - Takes a break (5)
19 - Makes brown (4)

Enter the letter in each circled cell in the order given below to reveal a themed answer:

13M	5B	2C	4E	4G	4J	6I	6A	7H	6K	10M	3K	5D	6G

11I

Clue: Who was the 29th Vice President and 30th President? (6,8)

Across

1 - Channels of the nose (8)
5 - Eg an arm or leg (4)
8 - Language of New Zealand (5)
9 - Not as old (7)
10 - Object used in the kitchen (7)
12 - Write again (7)
14 - Sideways looks (7)
16 - Impose one's will (7)
18 - Cheat; con (7)
19 - Scratchy (5)
20 - Read (anag) (4)
21 - Scaly anteater (8)

Down

1 - Title; label (4)
2 - Kept hold of (6)
3 - Fresh precipitation (9)
4 - Plan or design of something (6)
6 - Take into the body (of food) (6)
7 - Thieves (8)
11 - Improving (9)
12 - Freed from captivity (8)
13 - Continent (6)
14 - Swiss city (6)
15 - Annul (6)
17 - ___ Gosling: Canadian actor (4)

Enter the letter in each circled cell in the order given below to reveal a themed answer:

11K	9K	8A	12G	3E	13M	8K	3C	4G	8H	13L	6C	13I	3L

38

Clue: The Gold Rush of 1848-55 brought 300,000 people to which US state? (10)

Across

1 - Fleshes out unnecessarily (4)
3 - Telescope lens (8)
9 - Remolds (7)
10 - Double-reed instruments (5)
11 - Perform below expectation (12)
14 - Ground condensation (3)
16 - Clear of guilt (5)
17 - Move on snow runners (3)
18 - Intricate and confusing (12)
21 - Country once ruled by Papa Doc (5)
22 - Boastful behavior (7)
23 - Plan anew (8)
24 - Heavy metal (4)

Down

1 - Convince (8)
2 - Chopped finely (5)
4 - Positive answer (3)
5 - Fortunate; opportune (12)
6 - Changes gradually (7)
7 - Compass point (4)
8 - Branch of science that studies stars (12)
12 - Breed of dog originating in Wales (5)
13 - Timber for burning (8)
15 - Grew tired (7)
19 - Senseless (5)
20 - Singe (4)
22 - Flexible container (3)

Enter the letter in each circled cell in the order given below to reveal a themed answer:

10A	12G	13J	1J	6M	6E	9F	13H	9K	2E

Clue: Who was the first published female poet in North America? (4,9)

Across

1 - Monster that changes form during a full moon (8)
5 - Creative thought (4)
8 - Lawful (5)
9 - Aircraft control surface (7)
10 - Body of water (7)
12 - Present for acceptance (7)
14 - Decanting (7)
16 - Hawker (7)
18 - Establishment for making beer (7)
19 - One of ten equal parts: one-___ (5)
20 - Nervy (4)
21 - Goes before (8)

Down

1 - Large bump caused by injury (4)
2 - Excessively intricate or ornate (6)
3 - Cascade (9)
4 - Reveal (anag) (6)
6 - Relating to the upper side of an animal (6)
7 - Irritating (8)
11 - Emotionally disturbing (9)
12 - Tangible (8)
13 - Stefan ___ : former tennis number one (6)
14 - Request made to God (6)
15 - Pressed clothes (6)
17 - Therefore (4)

Enter the letter in each circled cell in the order given below to reveal a themed answer:

2E	8L	2M	1B	11A	6I	7A	9C	13M	11L	11B	11J	13A	4A

Clue: Which series of programs and reforms were enacted by Franklin D. Roosevelt between 1933 and 1936? (3,4)

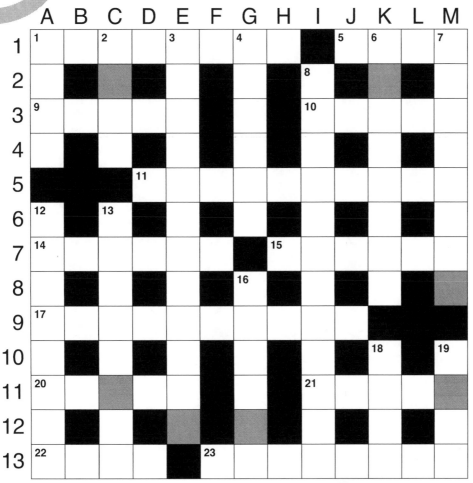

Across

1 - Without law or control (8)
5 - Not new (4)
9 - Mark ___ : Samuel Langhorne Clemens (5)
10 - Eg lunch and dinner (5)
11 - Fiendish (10)
14 - Complex problem (6)
15 - Small summerhouse (6)
17 - Supplementary (10)
20 - Keyboard instrument (5)
21 - Important question (5)
22 - Child's plaything (4)
23 - Mesmerism (8)

Down

1 - Social insects (4)
2 - First man (4)
3 - Verification (12)
4 - Drink (6)
6 - Looked for (8)
7 - Prohibit (8)
8 - Combination of companies into a single body (12)
12 - Renovated (8)
13 - Unexpected gain or advantage (8)
16 - Corporal (6)
18 - Queries (4)
19 - Animal doctors (4)

Enter the letter in each circled cell in the order given below to reveal a themed answer:

12E	2K	8M	2C	11M	11C	12G

41

Clue: Which group drafted the Declaration of Independence? (9,2,4)

Across

1 - Greases; lubricates (4)
3 - Country in southeastern Asia (8)
9 - Conceited person (7)
10 - Repository (5)
11 - Displeasure (12)
14 - Title for a Turkish military official (3)
16 - Freight carried on a ship (5)
17 - Seventh Greek letter (3)
18 - Completely devoted (12)
21 - Hot pepper (5)
22 - Permitted (7)
23 - Relating to the home (8)
24 - Salver (4)

Down

1 - Create an account deficit (8)
2 - Textile machines (5)
4 - What a painter produces (3)
5 - And also (12)
6 - Speculate (7)
7 - Performs in a play (4)
8 - Tricky elements; obstacles (12)
12 - Our planet (5)
13 - Frankly (8)
15 - Belief that there is no God (7)
19 - Tall narrow building (5)
20 - Dice (anag) (4)
22 - Muhammad ___ : boxer (3)

Enter the letter in each circled cell in the order given below to reveal a themed answer:

11A	1A	13C	4C	5J	3G	8G	9H	5G	13B	5E	5F	5B	2A

10C

42

Clue: Which British Prime Minister gave a eulogy at the funeral of President Reagan? (8,8)

Across

1 - ___ Chanel: French fashion designer (4)
3 - Astronaut (8)
9 - Seasonal prevailing wind (7)
10 - Pertaining to the ear (5)
11 - Supply with new weapons (5)
12 - Highest female singing voice (7)
13 - Irritating inconvenience (6)
15 - Opposite of top (6)
17 - Chats (7)
18 - European country (5)
20 - Where one finds Milan (5)
21 - Resemble (7)
22 - Relating to explanation (8)
23 - Volcano in Sicily (4)

Down

1 - Wide-ranging (13)
2 - Cuban dance (5)
4 - Subject to a penalty (6)
5 - Type of contest (12)
6 - Biting (7)
7 - Former President of South Africa (6,7)
8 - Preservative (12)
14 - Satisfy (7)
16 - Birthplace of St Francis (6)
19 - Modify (5)

Enter the letter in each circled cell in the order given below to reveal a themed answer:

1K	11C	4E	13D	1L	5J	2M	11J	7J	2I	7B	7K	1C	10E	11M	3K

43

Clue:Who was President whilst Walter Mondale was Vice President? (5,6)

Across

1 - Similarity (8)
5 - ___ Sharif: Egyptian actor (4)
8 - Expressing direct emotion (5)
9 - Called on (7)
10 - Follow a winding course (of a river) (7)
12 - ___ Joan Hart: US actress (7)
14 - Statement of transactions (7)
16 - Examined the quality of an ore (7)
18 - Massage technique (7)
19 - Go about stealthily (5)
20 - Takes an exam (4)
21 - Relating to meaning in language (8)

Down

1 - Bell-shaped flower (4)
2 - Inner part of a seed (6)
3 - Mandatory (9)
4 - Mark of disgrace (6)
6 - Get by with what is at hand (4,2)
7 - Send to a different place (8)
11 - Non-canonical religious texts (9)
12 - Thick dark syrup (8)
13 - Support; help (6)
14 - Command solemnly (6)
15 - Destroy (6)
17 - Group of countries joined by treaty (4)

Enter the letter in each circled cell in the order given below to reveal a themed answer:

10G	11C	5G	13H	10I	13M	2K	10K	13C	5C	12G

Clue: Who was Vice President when Bill Clinton was President? (2,4)

Across

1 - Ark builder (4)
3 - Bridgelike structures (8)
9 - Distant runner-up in a horse race (4-3)
10 - Willing type of attitude (3-2)
11 - Relating to numbers (12)
14 - Moderately dry (of champagne) (3)
16 - Consumed (of food) (5)
17 - Slender bristle of a grass (3)
18 - Limitless (12)
21 - Mature human (5)
22 - Gift (7)
23 - All people (8)
24 - Verge (4)

Down

1 - Narrowly avoided accident (4,4)
2 - Item of value (5)
4 - Charged particle (3)
5 - Lexicons (12)
6 - Musical composition (7)
7 - Long and laborious work (4)
8 - Without respect (12)
12 - Singing voices (5)
13 - Disturb (8)
15 - Calculate (7)
19 - Mix smoothly (5)
20 - Create (4)
22 - Writing instrument (3)

Enter the letter in each circled cell in the order given below to reveal a themed answer:

5G	12M	4M	2G	4E	2A

Clue: Which famous public speech did Martin Luther King Jr. give on 28 August 1963? (1,4,1,5)

Across

1 - Mocks (4)
3 - Natural homes of animals (8)
9 - Taught (7)
10 - Sumptuous meal (5)
11 - Person recovering from an illness (12)
13 - Of delicate beauty (6)
15 - Heed (6)
17 - Expensive clothes (5,7)
20 - Friend (Spanish) (5)
21 - Compels (7)
22 - Someone paddling a light boat (8)
23 - Not evens (4)

Down

1 - Come before (8)
2 - ___ John: pop star (5)
4 - Mixed up or confused (6)
5 - Contagiously (12)
6 - Contrary to (7)
7 - Hardens (4)
8 - Swimming technique (12)
12 - Opposites (8)
14 - Eg a resident of Rome (7)
16 - Thespians (6)
18 - Strongly advised (5)
19 - ___ Jacobs: US fashion designer (4)

Enter the letter in each circled cell in the order given below to reveal a themed answer:

11C	9B	3K	5D	6A	7B	3G	12G	4I	11A	11B

46

Clue: Which African-American literary and artistic movement developed in New York during the 1920s? (6,10)

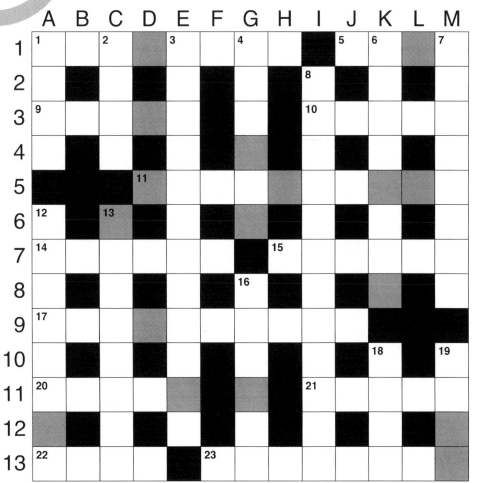

Across

1 - Relating to weather (8)
5 - Lose strength or effectiveness (4)
9 - Platforms leading out to sea (5)
10 - Principle of morality (5)
11 - Slightly unwell (10)
14 - Sayings (6)
15 - Furthest; extreme (6)
17 - Despotic (10)
20 - Small fruit used for oil (5)
21 - Paint (anag) (5)
22 - Dispatched (4)
23 - Of the highest quality (3-5)

Down

1 - Drinking vessels (4)
2 - Wild mountain goat (4)
3 - Lost in thought (12)
4 - Spain and Portugal (6)
6 - Attachment (8)
7 - Clarity (8)
8 - Prolongation (12)
12 - Feelings (8)
13 - Act of hard work (8)
16 - Alyssa ___ : US actress (6)
18 - Defer action (4)
19 - Engrave with acid (4)

Enter the letter in each circled cell in the order given below to reveal a themed answer:

13M	9D	3D	1L	11E	1D	4G	5L	8K	11G	5D	5K	5H	6G

12A	12M	6C

47

Clue: What was the name of the famous speech given by Sojourner Truth? (4,1,1,5)

Across

1 - Emperor of Rome 54-68 AD (4)
3 - Speaks softly (8)
9 - Birds eaten at Christmas (7)
10 - Huge (5)
11 - Electronic security device (7,5)
14 - Mythical monster (3)
16 - Sticks together (5)
17 - Soak up (3)
18 - Censure (12)
21 - Broadcast again (5)
22 - Japanese dish of raw fish (7)
23 - Social insect (8)
24 - Male deer (4)

Down

1 - Small portable computer (8)
2 - Less common (5)
4 - Ash (anag) (3)
5 - Altruism (12)
6 - Tympanic membrane (7)
7 - Vehicle on runners used on snow (4)
8 - Hostility (12)
12 - Rocky; harsh (5)
13 - Paying out money (8)
15 - V-shaped mark (7)
19 - Simpleton (5)
20 - Curved shape (4)
22 - Female person or animal (3)

Enter the letter in each circled cell in the order given below to reveal a themed answer:

5J	11K	9I	13K	6E	2G	1F	9L	7K	5H	12M

Clue: Established in 1607, what was the first permanent English settlement in North America? (9)

Across

1 - Hatred (6)
4 - Dung beetle (6)
9 - Finishing points (7)
10 - Shuns (7)
11 - Rafael ___ : Spanish tennis star (5)
12 - Moves back and forth (5)
14 - Performed on stage (5)
15 - Looks after oneself (5)
17 - Piece of code used to automate a task (5)
18 - Decorative narrow pieces of cloth (7)
20 - Organs (7)
21 - Deep sea inlets (6)
22 - Plan of action (6)

Down

1 - Expand in scope (6)
2 - Reduce the price of (4,4)
3 - Try out (5)
5 - Agreement (7)
6 - Speed contest (4)
7 - Explosions (6)
8 - Pleasant to think about but unrealistic (3,2,3,3)
13 - Specific; tangible (8)
14 - Shock with wonder (7)
15 - A long way away (3-3)
16 - Light spongy food (6)
17 - Doctor (5)
19 - Vigor (4)

Enter the letter in each circled cell in the order given below to reveal a themed answer:

13B	2C	13L	13M	4H	1E	2I	7C	10F

Clue: Who is the 45th US President? (6,5)

Across

1 - Long deep tracks (4)
3 - Went along (8)
9 - Disturb (7)
10 - Exhaust gases (5)
11 - Egotism (4-8)
14 - Plant juice (3)
16 - Customary (5)
17 - Fairy (3)
18 - Highly abstract (12)
21 - Army cloth (5)
22 - Plunder (7)
23 - Second largest ocean (8)
24 - Small fight (4)

Down

1 - Reevaluate (8)
2 - Tremulous sound (5)
4 - Foot part (3)
5 - Easily (12)
6 - Legal possession of land as one's own (7)
7 - Shallow food container (4)
8 - Surrender (12)
12 - Come into contact with (5)
13 - Flowing out (8)
15 - Be victorious (7)
19 - Brace (5)
20 - Gull-like bird (4)
22 - 21st Greek letter (3)

Enter the letter in each circled cell in the order given below to reveal a themed answer:

1M	4I	6K	3A	7I	1K	5G	5I	1B	9B	11G

Clue: 'The Feminine Mystique' was published in 1963 by which author? (5,7)

	A	B	C	D	E	F	G	H	I	J	K	L	M
1	1	2		3		4		5		6		7	
2													
3	8					9							
4													
5	10						11					12	
6						13							
7	14								15				
8													
9	16		17					18					
10							19						
11	20	21							22				
12													
13	23						24						

Across

1 - Part of a tree (6)
5 - Throngs (6)
8 - Prima donna (4)
9 - Move out of the way of (8)
10 - Stitched (5)
11 - Encode (7)
14 - Disloyalty (13)
16 - Country in North Europe (7)
18 - Urged on (5)
20 - Moderately rich; prosperous (4-2-2)
22 - Throw a coin in the air (4)
23 - Narrow drinking tubes (6)
24 - In prison (6)

Down

2 - Repeat (9)
3 - Closest (7)
4 - Person who receives guests (4)
5 - Pursuit of pleasure (8)
6 - Vertical part of a step (5)
7 - Female sheep (3)
12 - Owned (9)
13 - Having a striking beauty (8)
15 - Works against (7)
17 - Mediterranean island (5)
19 - ___ Berra: baseball player (4)
21 - Young newt (3)

Enter the letter in each circled cell in the order given below to reveal a themed answer:

1A	1L	8B	7D	5K	7A	1B	10F	5B	9A	3D	1D

51

Clue: Which battle of the American Revolutionary War, fought on 16 August 1780, saw a major victory for the British? (6)

Across

1 - Recording medium (4)
3 - Person who writes music (8)
9 - Stopped working (7)
10 - Kingdom (5)
11 - Fruit of the oak (5)
12 - Farthest away (7)
13 - Erase a mark from a surface (6)
15 - Sour to the taste (6)
17 - Plans (7)
18 - Gena Lee ___ : actress (5)
20 - Blunder (5)
21 - Reveal (7)
22 - Christmastide (8)
23 - Image of a god (4)

Down

1 - Menacingly (13)
2 - Paved area (5)
4 - More likely than not (4-2)
5 - Display of fireworks (12)
6 - Eg fish and shellfish (7)
7 - Device for changing TV channel (6,7)
8 - Exceptional (12)
14 - Portentous (7)
16 - Distributed (6)
19 - Cherished (5)

Enter the letter in each circled cell in the order given below to reveal a themed answer:

1F	2C	3M	9F	12G	6G

Clue: What is the term for the nationwide constitutional ban on the production and sale of alcohol from 1920 to 1933? (11)

Across

1 - Breaks (8)
5 - Country with capital Bamako (4)
8 - Type of wheat (5)
9 - Plumbing fixture (7)
10 - Be adequate (7)
12 - Ancient Egyptian ruler (7)
14 - Wrangled over price (7)
16 - Parched (7)
18 - Pit viper (7)
19 - Solid blow (5)
20 - Forefather (4)
21 - Act of accepting with approval (8)

Down

1 - Carbonated drink (4)
2 - Atmospheric phenomenon (6)
3 - Stencils (9)
4 - Recycle old material (6)
6 - Spiny tree (6)
7 - Fearless and brave (8)
11 - End of a digit (9)
12 - Decorative designs (8)
13 - Form of address for a man (6)
14 - Composite of different species (6)
15 - Lapis ___ : semiprecious stone (6)
17 - Puns (anag) (4)

Enter the letter in each circled cell in the order given below to reveal a themed answer:

13I	9D	13L	6B	13K	10G	12G	1E	13B	4C	12A

Clue: Which American dance originated in Harlem, New York City in 1928? (5,3)

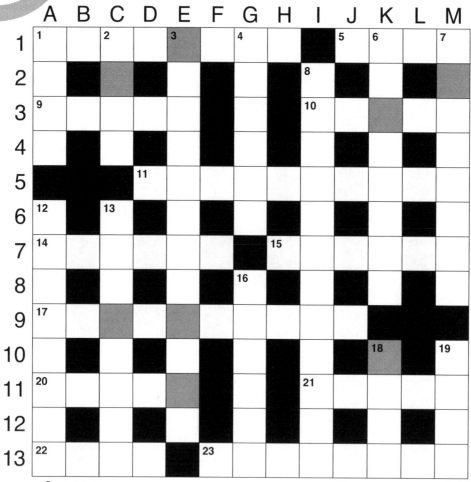

Across

1 - Formal curse by a pope (8)
5 - Capital of the Ukraine (4)
9 - Plantain lily (5)
10 - ___ DeGeneres: US comedienne (5)
11 - Eg cooking in a wok (4-6)
14 - One who belongs to a group (6)
15 - Shooting star (6)
17 - Downpour (10)
20 - Relay device (5)
21 - Show triumphant joy (5)
22 - Sell (anag) (4)
23 - Captive (8)

Down

1 - Having pains (4)
2 - Niche (4)
3 - Very upsetting (12)
4 - Adult (6)
6 - Inopportune (3-5)
7 - Sour (8)
8 - Bravery; boldness (12)
12 - Friendly (8)
13 - Everlasting (8)
16 - Street entertainer (6)
18 - Chinese monetary unit (4)
19 - Agitate; mix (4)

Enter the letter in each circled cell in the order given below to reveal a themed answer:

3K	2M	11E	9E	10K	1E	9C	2C

54

Clue: In 1870, who became the first African American to serve in the U.S. Congress? (5,6)

Across

1 - Smear or blur (6)
5 - Dutch spring flowers (6)
8 - Heroic tale (4)
9 - Elementary particle (8)
10 - Blows; hits swiftly (5)
11 - Substitute (7)
14 - Avoidance by going around (13)
16 - Large web-footed bird (7)
18 - ___ Arabia: country in the Middle East (5)
20 - Consignment (8)
22 - Italian acknowledgment (4)
23 - Bracelet for the foot (6)
24 - Attractive (6)

Down

2 - At the same time (9)
3 - Severe or serious (7)
4 - Saw; observed (4)
5 - Settlers (anag) (8)
6 - Language of the Romans (5)
7 - In favor of (3)
12 - Transmit a TV show (9)
13 - Inherent (8)
15 - Share; portion (7)
17 - Urge into action (5)
19 - Pace (4)
21 - Female chicken (3)

Enter the letter in each circled cell in the order given below to reveal a themed answer:

6B	11K	6L	9F	11E	13I	12B	7G	11F	8B	1M

55

Clue: Which English ship transported the Pilgrims from Plymouth, England to America in 1620? (9)

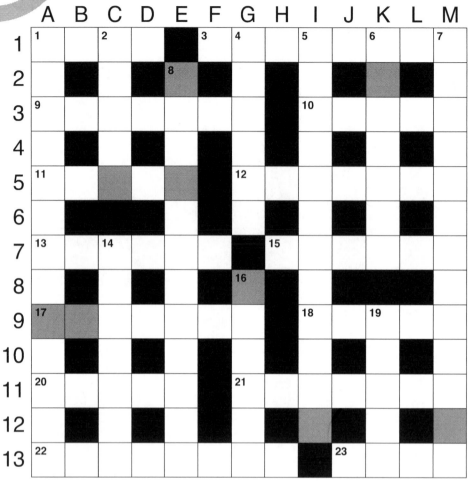

Across

1 - Make fun of (4)
3 - Very happy (8)
9 - Makes a journey (7)
10 - Temporary lodgings (5)
11 - Animal trimmings (5)
12 - Not listened to (7)
13 - Bodies of water (6)
15 - Fleet (6)
17 - Art of public speaking (7)
18 - Period of darkness (5)
20 - Type of expression (5)
21 - Opposite of pushing (7)
22 - Unable to appreciate music (4-4)
23 - Give a meal to (4)

Down

1 - One who studies the atmosphere and weather (13)
2 - Debris from threshing (5)
4 - Keep secret (4,2)
5 - Incomprehensibly (12)
6 - Brazilian dance (7)
7 - Deprived (13)
8 - Possessing sound knowledge (4-8)
14 - High spirits (7)
16 - Nearsightedness (6)
19 - Move effortlessly through air (5)

Enter the letter in each circled cell in the order given below to reveal a themed answer:

8G	2K	12I	5C	5E	9A	2E	12M	9B

56

Clue: Who was the first woman to hold federal office in the United States? (9,6)

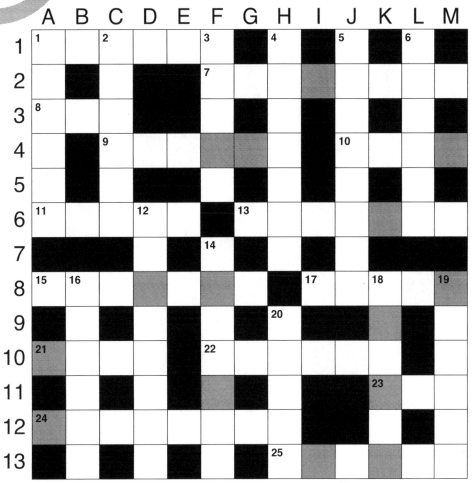

Across

1 - Refuses to obey (6)
7 - Leftovers; scraps (8)
8 - Jolt (3)
9 - Environment (6)
10 - Smooth and level (4)
11 - Heading (5)
13 - Object (7)
15 - Disgraceful event (7)
17 - Good at (5)
21 - Bean curd (4)
22 - Had a strong and unpleasant smell (6)
23 - Organ of sight (3)
24 - Tossing and catching items continuously (8)
25 - Deliberately catch out (6)

Down

1 - Dispirit (6)
2 - Size or style (6)
3 - Small branch (5)
4 - Get as one's own (7)
5 - Controlled; managed (8)
6 - Concurs (6)
12 - Tongue (8)
14 - Country in western Asia (7)
16 - Part of a song (6)
18 - Make beloved (6)
19 - Adjust for better efficiency (4-2)
20 - Threshold; brink (5)

Enter the letter in each circled cell in the order given below to reveal a themed answer:

12A	11K	8F	9K	13I	6K	8M	10A	4G	13K	11F	8D	2I	4F	4M

Clue: Who was President whilst Spiro Agnew was Vice President? (7,5)

Across

1 - Exaggerate (8)
5 - ___ Flynn Boyle: US actress (4)
8 - Formerly the Democratic Republic of the Congo (5)
9 - Atrocious act (7)
10 - Connected by kinship (7)
12 - Made something hard to perceive (7)
14 - Eg ape or human (7)
16 - Majestically (7)
18 - Angle of a compass bearing (7)
19 - Permit (5)
20 - TV award (4)
21 - Unjustly (8)

Down

1 - Greek spirit (4)
2 - Left (6)
3 - Existing in abundance (9)
4 - On a ship or train (6)
6 - Changes (6)
7 - Short account of an incident (8)
11 - State whose capital is Baton Rouge (9)
12 - Wedlock (8)
13 - Self-interest (6)
14 - Snake (6)
15 - Deer horn (6)
17 - Apart (4)

Enter the letter in each circled cell in the order given below to reveal a themed answer:

5G	6E	4M	11G	12M	8H	6C	13G	10A	2C	11L	9K

58

Clue: Which initiative, passed in 1948, sought to economically assist Western Europe? (8,4)

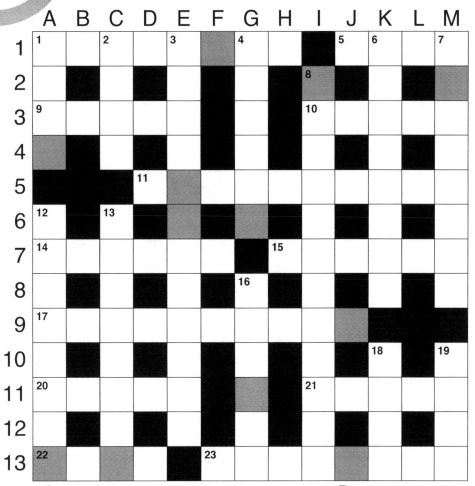

Across

1 - Inn (8)
5 - Applaud (4)
9 - Timepiece (5)
10 - Happen (5)
11 - Tracking dog (10)
14 - Mistakes (6)
15 - Current of air (6)
17 - Contemplation (10)
20 - Imitative of the past (5)
21 - Seabird deposit (5)
22 - Plant used to flavor food (4)
23 - Canine that herds animals (8)

Down

1 - Scream (4)
2 - Point of an occurrence (4)
3 - Feeling of great joy (12)
4 - Donors (anag) (6)
6 - Reproved formally (8)
7 - Mimics humorously (8)
8 - First language (6,6)
12 - Damage the reputation of (8)
13 - Animal that hunts (8)
16 - Join (6)
18 - Extol (4)
19 - Unpleasant smell (4)

Enter the letter in each circled cell in the order given below to reveal a themed answer:

2I	6E	13C	6G	13A	11G	1F	5E	13J	4A	2M	9J

59

Clue: Which acts were passed during the 1930s to ensure that the United States would not become involved in foreign conflicts? (10,4)

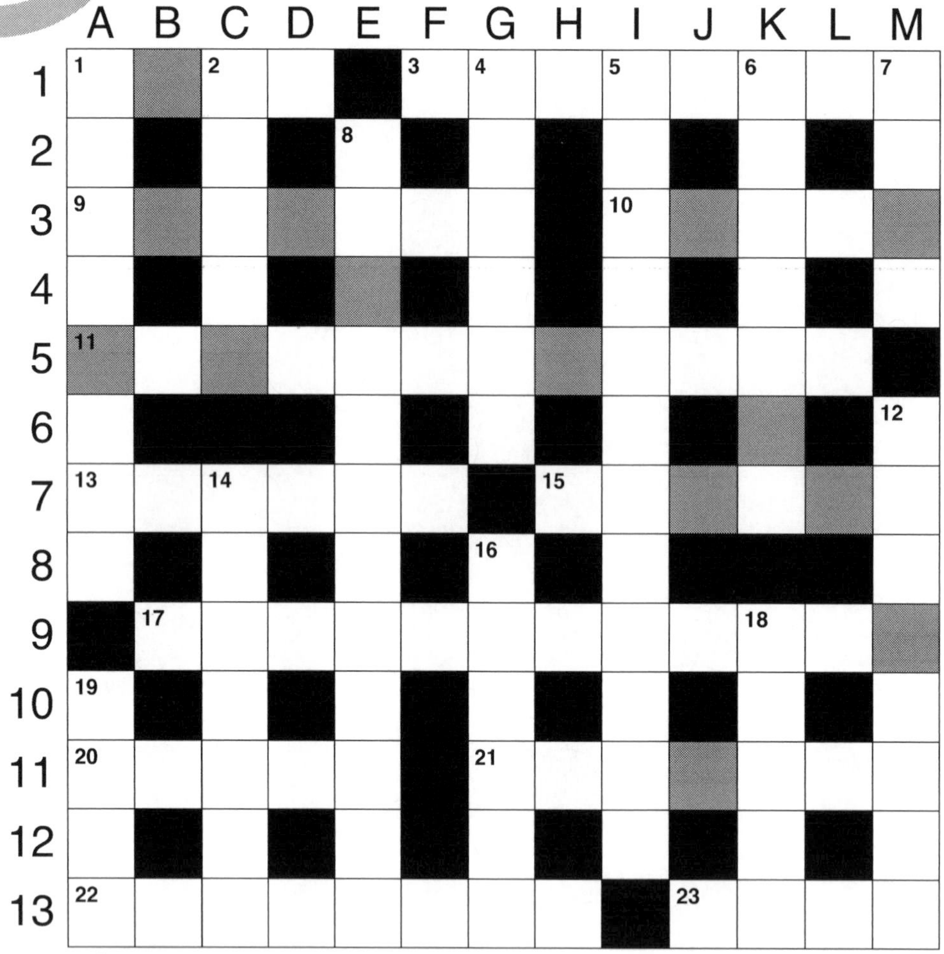

A B C D E F G H I J K L M

(crossword grid, rows 1–13)

Across

1 - Joined by stitches (4)
3 - Pledged to do (8)
9 - Handbook published annually (7)
10 - Female relatives (5)
11 - Scornful (12)
13 - Duty or tax (6)
15 - Rough shelter (4-2)
17 - Intuitively designed (of a system) (4-8)
20 - Body of rules; member of the clergy (5)
21 - Obedient (7)
22 - Spread out (8)
23 - Ill-mannered child (4)

Down

1 - Abrupt; disjointed (8)
2 - Lady (5)
4 - List of the constituents of a dish (6)
5 - Eg the size and length of something (12)
6 - Reddening of the skin (7)
7 - Office table (4)
8 - Disturbance (12)
12 - Multilingual (8)
14 - Begrudges (7)
16 - Women who are about to marry (6)
18 - Put off; delay (5)
19 - Race along (4)

Enter the letter in each circled cell in the order given below to reveal a themed answer:

5C	1B	3J	5H	6K	3D	3B	11J	4E	9M	7J	5A	7L	3M

Clue: Mark Twain and Charles Dudley Warner coined which term to describe the final three decades of the nineteenth-century? (6,3)

Across

1 - Separated seed from a plant (8)
5 - Assist (4)
9 - Of greater age (5)
10 - Picture (5)
11 - Advantageous (10)
14 - Permits (6)
15 - Consented (6)
17 - Uncultured person (10)
20 - Extent or limit (5)
21 - Not concealed (5)
22 - Cook slowly in liquid (4)
23 - A division in a group (8)

Down

1 - Golf pegs (4)
2 - Repeat an action (4)
3 - Creator of movie scripts (12)
4 - Item of stationery (6)
6 - Studied in detail (8)
7 - Make impossible (8)
8 - Insincere (12)
12 - Defensive walls (8)
13 - Association between countries (8)
16 - Style of slanting letters (6)
18 - Legendary creature (4)
19 - Amaze (4)

Enter the letter in each circled cell in the order given below to reveal a themed answer:

3L	5I	8C	8K	3M	2I	11B	7I	1G

Clue: In 1870, who became the first woman to vote in a general election in the United States? (6,5)

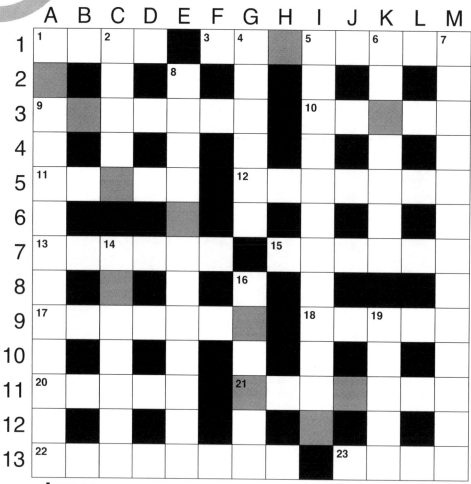

Across

1 - Small particle (4)
3 - Able to feel things (8)
9 - Signal to proceed (2-5)
10 - Tropical fruit (5)
11 - Stagnates (5)
12 - Stun gem (anag) (7)
13 - Take a firm stand (6)
15 - Tenant (6)
17 - Flowering shrubs (7)
18 - Titled (5)
20 - River cove; bay (5)
21 - Pancreatic hormone (7)
22 - Recently married person (8)
23 - Land surrounded by water (4)

Down

1 - Enlargement (13)
2 - Lag behind (5)
4 - Finish (6)
5 - Fellowship (12)
6 - Beautifies with a colorful surface (7)
7 - Existence beyond the physical level (13)
8 - Tenaciously; doggedly (12)
14 - Swift-flying songbird (7)
16 - Seek ambitiously (6)
19 - Shopping venues (5)

Enter the letter in each circled cell in the order given below to reveal a themed answer:

5C	3B	11J	11G	9G	3K	12I	8C	2A	6E	1H

62

Clue: Who was President whilst Alben Barkley was Vice President? (5,1,6)

Across

1 - ___ Macpherson: Australian supermodel (4)
3 - Country in Northeast Africa (8)
9 - Heading of an article (7)
10 - Camera image (abbrev.) (5)
11 - Characteristic of a past era (3-9)
14 - Consume food (3)
16 - Innate worth (5)
17 - Disapproving sound (3)
18 - Indifferent (12)
21 - Verse form (5)
22 - Nominal (7)
23 - Inclination (8)
24 - Moved quickly (4)

Down

1 - Surrounds on all sides (8)
2 - Fatty compound (5)
4 - Silvery-white metal (3)
5 - Enhancements (12)
6 - Saying (7)
7 - Long nerve fiber (4)
8 - Mishap (12)
12 - ___ Berry: actress (5)
13 - Thought curiously (8)
15 - Stress (7)
19 - Spring flower (5)
20 - Close (4)
22 - Twitch (3)

Enter the letter in each circled cell in the order given below to reveal a themed answer:

5G	6G	9H	6K	13H	5F	9K	4I	10K	8I	5E	13C

Clue: Having obtained statehood in 1959, what is the most recent state to have joined the United States? (6)

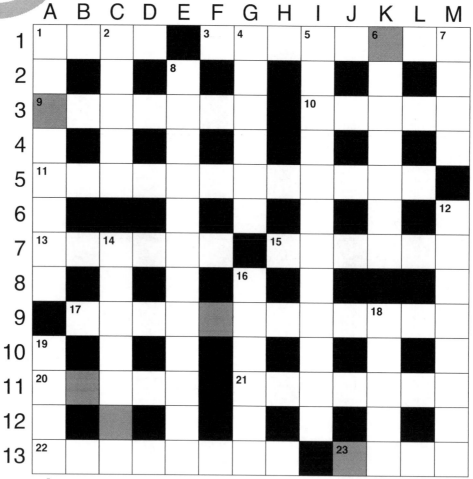

Across

1 - Distribute playing cards (4)
3 - People of no influence (8)
9 - Made less narrow (7)
10 - Consumer (5)
11 - Absurd (12)
13 - Takes the place of (6)
15 - Occupation or profession (6)
17 - Agreed upon by several parties (12)
20 - Pollex (5)
21 - Guards (7)
22 - Accepts to be true (8)
23 - Continent (4)

Down

1 - A heavy rain (8)
2 - Confuse (5)
4 - Eccentricity (6)
5 - Excessive response (12)
6 - Trespass (7)
7 - Ride the waves (4)
8 - Discordant (12)
12 - Formerly Ceylon (3,5)
14 - Uncommon (7)
16 - Leave the nest (6)
18 - Slopes (5)
19 - Tabs (anag) (4)

Enter the letter in each circled cell in the order given below to reveal a themed answer:

11B	13J	3A	12C	1K	9F

64

Clue: What was the term for the generation of young women in the 1920s who famously wore short skirts, listened to jazz and had bobbed hair styles? (8)

(Grid columns A B C D E F G H I J K L M, rows 1–13)

Across

1 - Source of inspiration (4)
3 - Wrinkled; creased (8)
9 - Not carrying weapons (7)
10 - Flexible insulated cables (5)
11 - Common greeting (5)
12 - Blood relationship (7)
13 - Self-supporting structures (6)
15 - Level plain without trees (6)
17 - Item of jewelry (7)
18 - Strength of a solution (5)
20 - Eg from Dublin (5)
21 - Eight-sided shape (7)
22 - Happiest (8)
23 - Sea eagle (4)

Down

1 - Tasty (5-8)
2 - Gastropod with a shell (5)
4 - John ____ : US novelist (6)
5 - Build up again from parts (12)
6 - Pay homage to (7)
7 - Evanescence (13)
8 - Made poor (12)
14 - Birthplace of Napoleon (7)
16 - Ice buildings (6)
19 - Big cat (5)

Enter the letter in each circled cell in the order given below to reveal a themed answer:

1F	5D	3C	2G	7K	9A	9C	7H

Clue: Established in 1585, what was the first English settlement in North America? (7,6)

Across

1 - Areas of skin irritation (6)
7 - Go past another car (8)
8 - Not on (3)
9 - Shapes in a fire (6)
10 - Entering (4)
11 - Rustic (5)
13 - Took along (7)
15 - Blotches (7)
17 - Bird homes (5)
21 - A brief piece of film (4)
22 - Tolerate something (6)
23 - Male sheep (3)
24 - According (8)
25 - Personify (6)

Down

1 - Troublemaker (6)
2 - Experience pain (6)
3 - Wet (5)
4 - Express severe disapproval of (7)
5 - Manner (8)
6 - Rough drawing (6)
12 - Believed to be true (8)
14 - Arch enemy (7)
16 - Assert without proof (6)
18 - Type of sound system (6)
19 - Decorous; proper (6)
20 - Saying (5)

Enter the letter in each circled cell in the order given below to reveal a themed answer:

6A	4D	1B	8I	3A	2L	10K	1H	13K	6E	6I	12G	5F

Clue: Which skyscraper was the world's tallest building before it was surpassed by the Empire State Building? (8,8)

Across

1 - Common name for sodium chloride (4)
3 - Reads out (8)
9 - Increase in size (7)
10 - Worked steadily at (5)
11 - Intensely painful (12)
14 - Toward the stern (3)
16 - Data entered (5)
17 - Herb (3)
18 - State of the USA (12)
21 - Textile weave (5)
22 - Duty-bound (7)
23 - New York (3,5)
24 - Walked or stepped (4)

Down

1 - Emaciated (8)
2 - Sweet-scented shrub (5)
4 - Era (anag) (3)
5 - Monotonously (12)
6 - Narrower (7)
7 - Froth of soap and water (4)
8 - A type of error in speech (8,4)
12 - Suggest (5)
13 - Recompensed; gave a gift to (8)
15 - Abounding (7)
19 - African country which has Niamey as its capital (5)
20 - Remnant of a pencil (4)
22 - Nocturnal bird of prey (3)

Enter the letter in each circled cell in the order given below to reveal a themed answer:

5F	2K	5D	9G	10E	1C	2I	1H	11H	5E	11C	4A	13M	11J

4K	13C

Clue: Which US policy of opposing European colonialism in the Americas was expressed in 1823? (6,8)

Across

1 - Total spread of a bridge (4)
3 - Needs (8)
9 - Philosophical theory (7)
10 - Lover of Juliet (5)
11 - Inflexible (12)
13 - Senior monks (6)
15 - Land holding (6)
17 - Formal notice (12)
20 - Floating platforms (5)
21 - Freezing (3-4)
22 - Excited commotion (8)
23 - Extremely (4)

Down

1 - State of remaining alive (8)
2 - Be in store (5)
4 - Entangle (6)
5 - True redesign (anag) (12)
6 - European country (7)
7 - Finish (4)
8 - Ruinously (12)
12 - Angrily (8)
14 - Destructive (7)
16 - Dark blue dye (6)
18 - Decay (5)
19 - Child's bed (4)

Enter the letter in each circled cell in the order given below to reveal a themed answer:

9J	11K	9L	13L	7D	3B	11M	3M	10A	8I	11A	8G	9D	4I

Clue: Who was the 44th US President? (6,5)

Across

1 - Manure (4)
3 - Absurd (8)
9 - Apprehend (7)
10 - Chilly (5)
11 - Lack of practical knowledge (12)
14 - Floor covering (3)
16 - Gold block (5)
17 - 19th Greek letter (3)
18 - Laudatory (12)
21 - With a forward motion (5)
22 - Exchange as part payment for something new (5,2)
23 - Our galaxy (5,3)
24 - Depend upon (4)

Down

1 - Exaggerated masculinity (8)
2 - Small woodland (5)
4 - Primate (3)
5 - In accordance with general custom (12)
6 - Imitator (7)
7 - Puts down (4)
8 - Shockingly (12)
12 - Scoundrel (5)
13 - Tendency to float in a fluid (8)
15 - Tumult (7)
19 - Subject; topic (5)
20 - Soothing remedy (4)
22 - Popular beverage (3)

Enter the letter in each circled cell in the order given below to reveal a themed answer:

6M	1G	11H	6K	3A	1D	11C	10A	13G	12K	2M

69

Clue: Which event ended the Vietnam War in 1975? (4,2,6)

Across

1 - Long mountain chain (6)
7 - Plant (8)
8 - By way of (3)
9 - Push forward (6)
10 - Driving shaft (4)
11 - Happening (5)
13 - Inflexible (7)
15 - Impresario (7)
17 - Enlighten; educate (5)
21 - Bathroom powder (abbrev.) (4)
22 - Breakfast cereal (6)
23 - Metal container (3)
24 - Capital of Finland (8)
25 - Far away from home (6)

Down

1 - Untamed (6)
2 - Pass by (of time) (6)
3 - Unconditional love (5)
4 - Introductory performance (7)
5 - Unscathed (8)
6 - Lightweight cotton cloth (6)
12 - Radio or TV broadcast (8)
14 - Remittance (7)
16 - Warmed up (6)
18 - Frozen water spear (6)
19 - Showed tiredness (6)
20 - Aimed (anag) (5)

Enter the letter in each circled cell in the order given below to reveal a themed answer:

13I	6I	13L	10J	8C	8L	8A	1F	8K	2F	4E	6D

Clue: Which US President issued the Emancipation Proclamation? (7,7)

Across

1 - Use something to maximum advantage (8)
5 - Look at amorously (4)
8 - Disturb (5)
9 - Having a mournful quality (7)
10 - Believe tentatively (7)
12 - Periods of 60 seconds (7)
14 - Branch of mathematics (7)
16 - Seminar (anag) (7)
18 - Shine brightly (7)
19 - ___ Els: golfer (5)
20 - Logical division (4)
21 - Impressions (8)

Down

1 - Noisy (4)
2 - Sight (6)
3 - Act of keeping in memory (9)
4 - Metamorphic rock (6)
6 - Showed around (6)
7 - And so on (2,6)
11 - Tiniest (9)
12 - Central American monkey (8)
13 - Wrinkle (6)
14 - Go up (6)
15 - Mustang (6)
17 - Chief god of ancient Greece (4)

Enter the letter in each circled cell in the order given below to reveal a themed answer:

9B	8K	8L	8M	9I	8G	6A	6I	6B	2G	12K	1J	8H	9E

Clue: In 1983, who became the first American woman in space? (5,4)

Across

1 - Remove silt from a river (6)
4 - Ancient Persian king (6)
9 - Nerve impulses (7)
10 - Existing in name only (7)
11 - Type of military operation (5)
12 - Leaves (5)
14 - Leans at an angle (5)
15 - Tropical tree native to South America (5)
17 - Utter; turn suddenly (5)
18 - Huge wave (7)
20 - Firmly; closely (7)
21 - Devices that tell the time (6)
22 - Gazed (6)

Down

1 - Cease (6)
2 - Large outbreak of a disease (8)
3 - Measuring instrument (5)
5 - Foes (7)
6 - Superhero film based on comic characters (1-3)
7 - Witches cast these (6)
8 - Peculiarity (11)
13 - Person who puts money into something (8)
14 - Fusion chamber (7)
15 - ___ acid: this is found in lemons (6)
16 - Entreated; beseeched (6)
17 - Vision (5)
19 - Reverse (4)

Enter the letter in each circled cell in the order given below to reveal a themed answer:

10K	8G	4M	3F	11M	1B	4J	1A	12M

72

Clue: Harriet Beecher Stowe published which anti-slavery novel in 1852? (5,4,5)

Across

1 - Unfavorable (8)
5 - Edible fruit (4)
9 - Faithful (5)
10 - These protect you from rain (5)
11 - Triumphant (10)
14 - Flattened at the poles (6)
15 - Trigonometrical ratio (6)
17 - The very early morning (5,5)
20 - City in Florida (5)
21 - Sprite (5)
22 - Facts and statistics (4)
23 - Plump (4-4)

Down

1 - Unattractive (4)
2 - Playthings (4)
3 - Small portable radio (6-6)
4 - Scarcity (6)
6 - Profitable (8)
7 - Held out against (8)
8 - Art of planning a dance (12)
12 - Ate (8)
13 - Agreeable (8)
16 - Anthropoid ape (6)
18 - Exhibition (4)
19 - Impose a tax (4)

Enter the letter in each circled cell in the order given below to reveal a themed answer:

5L	10G	2I	13H	6I	6M	2C	11A	5M	8K	13D	7B	11E	7L

Clue: The 1960 novel 'To Kill a Mockingbird' was the recipient of which literary prize? (8,5)

Across

1 - Head coverings (4)
3 - Unwanted correspondence (4,4)
9 - Grows larger (7)
10 - Administrative capital of Bolivia (2,3)
11 - Middleman (12)
13 - Seeping (6)
15 - Humorous blunder (6)
17 - Flaw (12)
20 - In what place (5)
21 - Removed the contents (7)
22 - Playful (8)
23 - Sight organs (4)

Down

1 - Person owed money (8)
2 - Songbird (5)
4 - Invisible (6)
5 - Children's toy (12)
6 - Clothing (7)
7 - Slothful (4)
8 - Action of breaking a law (12)
12 - Explosive shells (8)
14 - River in Africa (7)
16 - Makes available for sale (6)
18 - Coldly (5)
19 - Woes (anag) (4)

Enter the letter in each circled cell in the order given below to reveal a themed answer:

1C	1G	3I	1L	9J	3M	11L	5K	3C	5E	9B	7C	6K

Clue: Which American baseball player was nicknamed 'the Bambino' and 'the Sultan of Swat'? (4,4)

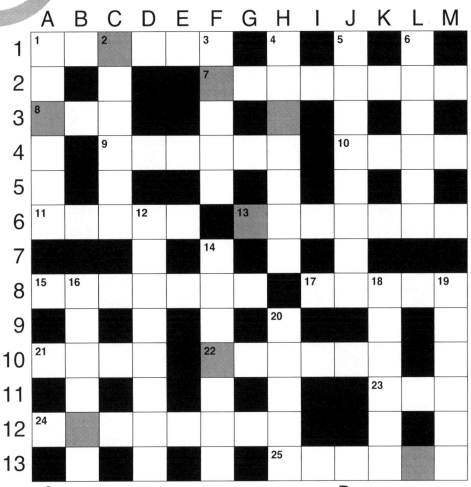

Across

1 - Yellowish-brown color (6)

7 - Unsubstantiated (8)

8 - ___ Ivanovic: Serbian tennis star (3)

9 - Unimportant facts (6)

10 - Center (4)

11 - Equip (5)

13 - Informs on (7)

15 - Decline (7)

17 - Academy award (5)

21 - Photographic material (4)

22 - Joins together (6)

23 - Range of vision (3)

24 - Move to another place (8)

25 - Juveniles (6)

Down

1 - Rarely encountered (6)

2 - Overjoyed (6)

3 - Opposite of below (5)

4 - Holdings; farms (7)

5 - Signs for public display (8)

6 - Far from the intended target (6)

12 - Approaching (8)

14 - Envelops (7)

16 - Regime (anag) (6)

18 - Small box (6)

19 - Competition stages (6)

20 - Intensely ardent (5)

Enter the letter in each circled cell in the order given below to reveal a themed answer:

2F	3A	6G	1C	12B	10F	3H	13L

Clue: Which failed military invasion of Cuba took place on 17-20 April 1961? (3,2,5)

Across

1 - Fall slowly (of water) (4)
3 - Progresses (8)
9 - Skills (7)
10 - Destiny; fate (5)
11 - Style of playing blues (6-6)
13 - Yells (6)
15 - Not singular (6)
17 - Fairly (12)
20 - Punch (5)
21 - Aromatic herb (7)
22 - Writer of literary works (8)
23 - Basic unit of an element (4)

Down

1 - Structured set of information (8)
2 - Ice house (5)
4 - Renounce; repudiate (6)
5 - Generally accepted (12)
6 - Bearer (7)
7 - ___ Penn: actor (4)
8 - Dimly; not clearly (12)
12 - Recreational area for children (8)
14 - Easily seen (7)
16 - Very well known (6)
18 - Preliminary sketch or version (5)
19 - Throb (4)

Enter the letter in each circled cell in the order given below to reveal a themed answer:

5A	11K	9M	12M	12K	7H	2E	10I	1M

Clue: What was the surname of the first Vice President of the United States? (5)

Across

1 - Face (anag) (4)
3 - Partial shadow (8)
9 - Low-lying areas of land (7)
10 - Shaped like a volcano (5)
11 - Type of verse (5)
12 - Threw away (7)
13 - Move or travel hurriedly (6)
15 - Concealed from view (6)
17 - One of the planets (7)
18 - Greek fabulist (5)
20 - Cake decoration (5)
21 - Quick musical tempo (7)
22 - Mathematically aware (8)
23 - Arthur ___ : former US tennis player (4)

Down

1 - Understanding (13)
2 - Sudden attack (5)
4 - Substitute (6)
5 - Unkind; unsympathetic (12)
6 - Clustered together (7)
7 - Liable to get injured often (8-5)
8 - Fast food item (12)
14 - Clever but false argument (7)
16 - Leave (6)
19 - Road information boards (5)

Enter the letter in each circled cell in the order given below to reveal a themed answer:

5I	5M	1M	13C	10A

Clue: 'The Gospel of Wealth' was an article written by which business magnate in June 1889? (6,8)

Across
1 - Canine shelter (8)
5 - Stylish (4)
8 - Pretend (5)
9 - Comments (7)
10 - Venetian boat (7)
12 - Uncovered (7)
14 - Hearing range (7)
16 - Dessert (anag) (7)
18 - Pasta pockets (7)
19 - Sauce that accompanies a roast (5)
20 - Young men (4)
21 - Explosive (8)

Down
1 - Skillful (4)
2 - Acquired (6)
3 - Decorations (9)
4 - Shows indifference (6)
6 - Agricultural implement (6)
7 - Percussion instrument (8)
11 - Intense type of pain (9)
12 - Relating to the coast (8)
13 - Moved repeatedly from side to side (6)
14 - Nervously (6)
15 - Honolulu is the capital of this state (6)
17 - Extravagant publicity (4)

Enter the letter in each circled cell in the order given below to reveal a themed answer:

2K	13H	13F	4K	7M	6K	1J	9K	9B	7E	12C	5G	7A	8G

78

Clue: To date, who was the only Roman Catholic President of the United States? (4,1,7)

Across

1 - Part of a dress (6)
4 - Place of refuge (6)
9 - Let go of (7)
10 - Evergreen conifer (7)
11 - Misty (5)
12 - Pains (5)
14 - Dangers (5)
15 - Tie; snag (5)
17 - One who avoids animal products (5)
18 - Bathing tub with bubbles (7)
20 - Gently (7)
21 - Locked lips with another (6)
22 - Spiritual meeting (6)

Down

1 - Deprived of (6)
2 - Industrious (8)
3 - Mad (5)
5 - Pete ___ : former tennis player (7)
6 - Reside (4)
7 - Church services (6)
8 - Inevitably (11)
13 - Increase (8)
14 - Underground plant stem (7)
15 - Illegally seize (6)
16 - Biochemical catalyst (6)
17 - Not clearly stated (5)
19 - Gear wheels (4)

Enter the letter in each circled cell in the order given below to reveal a themed answer:

10A	11E	8E	9M	5A	13A	9J	2G	7C	8M	1C	5E

79

Clue: Which banned American novel was the subject of an obscenity trial in the United Kingdom in 1960? (4,11,5)

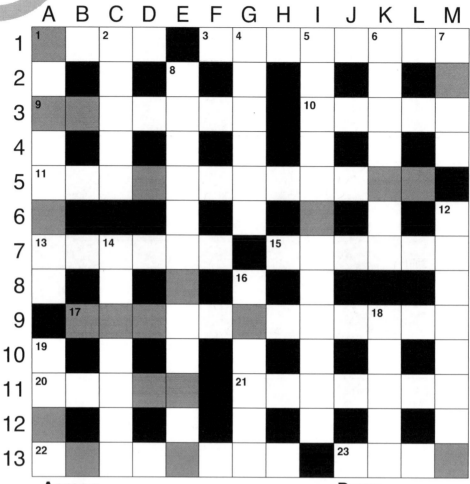

Across

- 1 - Be at a ___ : be puzzled (4)
- 3 - Assisting the memory (8)
- 9 - Knot or coil of hair (7)
- 10 - Rope with a running noose (5)
- 11 - Understandably (12)
- 13 - Marked by friendly companionship (6)
- 15 - Less tame (6)
- 17 - Beneficial (12)
- 20 - Fly an airplane (5)
- 21 - Dandier (anag) (7)
- 22 - A period of 366 days (4,4)
- 23 - Inheritor (4)

Down

- 1 - Most fortunate (8)
- 2 - Move (5)
- 4 - Papal representative (6)
- 5 - Knowing more than one language (12)
- 6 - Settled oneself comfortably (7)
- 7 - Plant yield (4)
- 8 - Nastily (12)
- 12 - Campaigner (8)
- 14 - Diacritical mark (7)
- 16 - Sporting arenas (6)
- 18 - Unit of weight (5)
- 19 - Gemstone (4)

Enter the letter in each circled cell in the order given below to reveal a themed answer:

5K	9B	9C	5L	3A	3B	12A	9G	11E	13B	2M	6I	5D	13E

8E	1A	11D	9D	6A	13M

80

Clue: Which peace treaty ended the Mexican-American war in 1848? (9,7)

Across

1 - Protect from harm (8)
5 - Sums together (4)
9 - Principle or belief (5)
10 - Atmospheric disturbance (5)
11 - Pieces of text beginning on new lines (10)
14 - Control; regulate (6)
15 - Quick look (6)
17 - Study of earthquakes (10)
20 - Eg a Martian (5)
21 - Light crinkled fabric (5)
22 - Spiritual and ascetic discipline (4)
23 - Putting into practice (8)

Down

1 - Reduces in length (4)
2 - Not any of (4)
3 - Separation (12)
4 - Roman god of fire (6)
6 - Letting go of (8)
7 - Part of an academic year (8)
8 - Relating to horoscopes (12)
12 - Person sent on a special mission (8)
13 - Tempting (8)
16 - Make a photographic enlargement of (4,2)
18 - Tractor-trailer (4)
19 - Mass of floating ice (abbrev.) (4)

Enter the letter in each circled cell in the order given below to reveal a themed answer:

13M	2A	7J	1L	5E	13I	12G	11L	2M	5L	13K	1K	11A	7I

13C	13B

Clue: The Salem witch trials of 1692-3 took place in which modern-day US state? (13)

Across

1 - Break apart suddenly (4)
3 - Surround (8)
9 - Tardiest (7)
10 - Vault under a church (5)
11 - Denial (12)
14 - Small spot (3)
16 - Rub out (5)
17 - ___ out: get with great difficulty (3)
18 - Interpret wrongly (12)
21 - Dissatisfaction; boredom (5)
22 - Type of sugar (7)
23 - Moved to tears (8)
24 - Resistance units (4)

Down

1 - Straddle (8)
2 - Open disrespect (5)
4 - Item dividing a tennis court in two (3)
5 - Ineptness (12)
6 - Hot pepper (7)
7 - Consumes food (4)
8 - Profitable (12)
12 - Grasp tightly (5)
13 - Unnecessary (8)
15 - Paired (7)
19 - Period of time (5)
20 - Untidy state (4)
22 - Observe (3)

Enter the letter in each circled cell in the order given below to reveal a themed answer:

9B	7G	3F	13M	2K	11I	9J	1B	13A	13G	5L	4A	1C

Clue: Which establishment sold alcoholic beverages during the Prohibition era? (9)

Across

1 - Funny TV show (6)
4 - Investor (6)
9 - Sharp organ of a wasp or bee (7)
10 - Formally approved (7)
11 - Dole out (5)
12 - Command (5)
14 - Sediment (5)
15 - Chunk (5)
17 - Earth (5)
18 - Copy (7)
20 - Exposes (7)
21 - Very small (6)
22 - Messengers of God (6)

Down

1 - Relaxed and unconcerned (6)
2 - Core mass of a country (8)
3 - A finger or toe (5)
5 - With reference to (7)
6 - Intertwined segment of rope (4)
7 - Cause to become (6)
8 - Disjointed; in pieces (11)
13 - Bleak; stark (8)
14 - Please immensely (7)
15 - Stretch prior to exercise (4,2)
16 - Extravagant meals (6)
17 - Acknowledged; assumed (5)
19 - Vegetable matter used as fuel (4)

Enter the letter in each circled cell in the order given below to reveal a themed answer:

3A	13A	7G	6C	1K	3F	13H	7I	1F

Clue: Which US President famously challenged Mikhail Gorbachev to 'tear down this wall!' in a speech in West Berlin? (6,6)

Across

1 - Pull a sulky face (4)
3 - People who place bets (8)
9 - Unconventional (7)
10 - Airship (5)
11 - Quantitative relation between amounts (5)
12 - First (7)
13 - Not dense (6)
15 - Shining (6)
17 - Turns upside down (7)
18 - Anemic looking (5)
20 - White water bird (5)
21 - Spiny anteater (7)
22 - Providing (8)
23 - Catch sight of (4)

Down

1 - Increasingly (13)
2 - Unsuitable (5)
4 - Reach; achieve (6)
5 - List of books referred to (12)
6 - Building (7)
7 - Additional (13)
8 - Showed (12)
14 - In an opposing direction (7)
16 - Behind a ship (6)
19 - Conceals (5)

Enter the letter in each circled cell in the order given below to reveal a themed answer:

12G	3A	6E	7H	12A	2E	9E	12K	9I	13H	11M	2C

84

Clue: Which style of art and architecture peaked during the Roaring Twenties? (3,4)

Across

1 - Avoided (6)
5 - Capacity (6)
8 - Examine quickly (4)
9 - Access code (8)
10 - Deprive of possessions (5)
11 - Mean; ordinary or usual (7)
14 - Things that are given (13)
16 - Guardians (7)
18 - Ghost (5)
20 - Improbable (8)
22 - Self-contained item (4)
23 - Tiny bits of bread (6)
24 - Senior members of tribes (6)

Down

2 - Careers; callings (9)
3 - One who works with teeth (7)
4 - Delude (4)
5 - Volcano near Naples (8)
6 - Bring down (5)
7 - Spoil (3)
12 - Venetian boatman (9)
13 - Pain or anguish (8)
15 - Seize and take legal custody of (7)
17 - Disgust (5)
19 - Sort (4)
21 - Boolean operator (3)

Enter the letter in each circled cell in the order given below to reveal a themed answer:

4B	9E	10H	13J	1A	9C	7K

Clue: What was the first battle of the American Civil War? (4,6)

Across

1 - Huge desert in North Africa (6)
7 - Ominous (8)
8 - Belonging to him (3)
9 - Drowsy (6)
10 - Deserve (4)
11 - Endures (5)
13 - Unfasten (7)
15 - Inventor (7)
17 - Hits high up in the air (5)
21 - Less than average tide (4)
22 - Frank (6)
23 - ___ Thurman: actress (3)
24 - Moving mechanical devices (8)
25 - Lacking warmth; bleak (6)

Down

1 - Place of education (6)
2 - Boos and ... (6)
3 - Stare (anag) (5)
4 - Wanting what someone else has (7)
5 - Starlike symbol (8)
6 - A system of measurement (6)
12 - Unit of measure in cookery (8)
14 - Hide (7)
16 - Expressing regret (6)
18 - Admit formally (6)
19 - Passionate (6)
20 - Relation by marriage (2-3)

Enter the letter in each circled cell in the order given below to reveal a themed answer:

11B	5A	13L	8E	6C	11K	12E	12C	10M	1E

Clue: Who was the only President to serve two non-consecutive terms in office? (6,9)

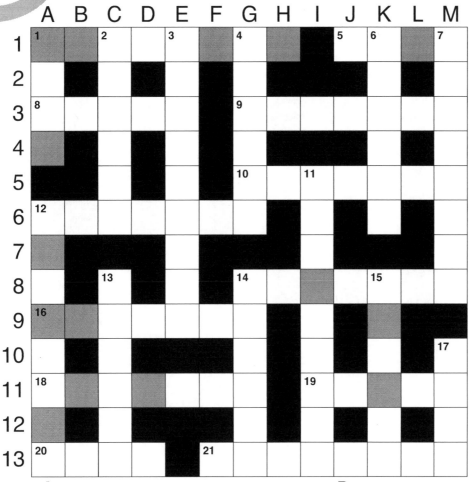

Across

1 - Upright (8)
5 - Brown seaweed (4)
8 - Lazed (5)
9 - Exploit to excess (7)
10 - Methods (7)
12 - Senior clergyman (7)
14 - Larval amphibian (7)
16 - ___ Hudgens: US actress (7)
18 - Guard (7)
19 - Creative thoughts (5)
20 - Strongbox (4)
21 - Evaluator (8)

Down

1 - Futile (4)
2 - Recount (6)
3 - Shows (9)
4 - Wake (someone) from sleep (6)
6 - Dodged (6)
7 - Feeling of enjoyment (8)
11 - Split into pieces (9)
12 - Supplies with (8)
13 - Unique (3-3)
14 - Pollutes (6)
15 - Female monster (6)
17 - Sure (anag) (4)

Enter the letter in each circled cell in the order given below to reveal a themed answer:

9K	11D	11B	1A	1B	7A	1F	1L	12A	9A	11K	1H	9B	4A

8I

87

Clue: Which protest, led by the Sons of Liberty, took place on 16 December 1773? (6,3,5)

Across

1 - Lifeless (8)

5 - Greek god of love (4)

9 - Juicy fruit (5)

10 - Nosed (anag) (5)

11 - Presidential residence (5,5)

14 - Small shellfish (6)

15 - Tricked (6)

17 - Diplomatic official (10)

20 - Natural yellow resin (5)

21 - Largely aquatic carnivorous mammal (5)

22 - Eg December 24 and 31 (4)

23 - Exempt from tax (4-4)

Down

1 - Short note (abbrev.) (4)

2 - Tough outer layer (4)

3 - Science of biological processes (12)

4 - Subtle detail (6)

6 - Intensify; strengthen (8)

7 - Hangs (8)

8 - Study of human societies (12)

12 - Increase rapidly (8)

13 - Likely to occur (8)

16 - Cake (6)

18 - Heavenly body (4)

19 - Release (4)

Enter the letter in each circled cell in the order given below to reveal a themed answer:

9C	4K	5L	5G	1B	1G	10E	11D	11A	4M	9A	11E	11J	13I

Clue: Who was Vice President from 1989-1993? (3,6)

Across

1 - Woodwind instrument (4)
3 - Pertaining to education (8)
9 - Tall tower (7)
10 - Sea nymph (5)
11 - Graphical (12)
13 - Get off (6)
15 - Two-piece bathing suit (6)
17 - Significantly (12)
20 - Reason for innocence (5)
21 - Not the same (7)
22 - Relight a fire (8)
23 - Farewells (4)

Down

1 - Glass-like volcanic rock (8)
2 - Drama set to music (5)
4 - Very milky (6)
5 - Displeased (12)
6 - Type of cocktail (7)
7 - Walking stick (4)
8 - Foreboding (12)
12 - Two-wheeled vehicles (8)
14 - Hand tool ending in a spike (3-4)
16 - Straighten out (6)
18 - Very bad (5)
19 - Animal's den (4)

Enter the letter in each circled cell in the order given below to reveal a themed answer:

5A	4G	3M	11J	11G	5I	9M	7B	13L

Clue: Which American singer was the first woman to achieve five number-one singles from one album? (4,5)

Across

1 - Assignment given to a student (8)
5 - Wireless transmission of data (2-2)
8 - Military trainee (5)
9 - Quick look (7)
10 - Forbidden by law (7)
12 - Person of high position within a group (7)
14 - Whenever (7)
16 - Having one set of chromosomes (7)
18 - Connection (7)
19 - Sheltered places (5)
20 - Indian dress (4)
21 - Engravings (8)

Down

1 - Access illegally (4)
2 - Make angry (6)
3 - Sport played in a pool (5,4)
4 - Recover (6)
6 - Cast doubt upon (6)
7 - Romanticize (8)
11 - Maze (9)
12 - Holy seek (anag) (8)
13 - First contest of a series (6)
14 - Arrival (6)
15 - Innate (6)
17 - Egyptian goddess (4)

Enter the letter in each circled cell in the order given below to reveal a themed answer:

6A	4G	13G	8A	6E	2G	5E	13C	8I

90

Clue: What was the middle name of President Nixon? (7)

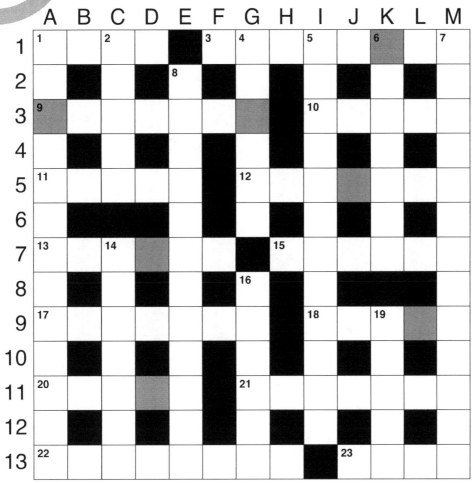

Across

1 - Team (4)
3 - Break (8)
9 - Four-legged reptiles (7)
10 - Avoid (5)
11 - Gave up power (5)
12 - Long distance postal service (7)
13 - Someone shirking duty (2-4)
15 - Travelers on horseback (6)
17 - Surpass (7)
18 - Vietnamese capital (5)
20 - Country in Western Asia (5)
21 - Employment vacancy (7)
22 - Intensified (8)
23 - Wet with condensation (4)

Down

1 - Openly acknowledged by oneself (4-9)
2 - Bewildered (5)
4 - Mischievous person (6)
5 - Thinking sensibly (5-7)
6 - Oblivious to (7)
7 - Eternally (13)
8 - Highest or first position (5,2,5)
14 - Spend lavishly (7)
16 - Indicate (6)
19 - Sound of any kind (5)

Enter the letter in each circled cell in the order given below to reveal a themed answer:

5J	11D	3A	7D	9L	1K	3G

Clue: Which battle of May 1865 has been cited as the final battle of the American Civil War? (7,5)

Across

1 - Liquids which dissolve other substances (8)
5 - Sage (anag) (4)
8 - Old object (5)
9 - Rice dish (7)
10 - Thinks curiously (7)
12 - Forward rotation of a ball (7)
14 - Guarantees (7)
16 - Painters (7)
18 - Reluctance to change (7)
19 - Porcelain (5)
20 - Breathe convulsively (4)
21 - Heavenly (8)

Down

1 - Arrange systematically (4)
2 - Move with a bounding motion (6)
3 - Surround (9)
4 - Unseated by a horse (6)
6 - Water channel (6)
7 - Financial backers (8)
11 - Bothersome people (9)
12 - Pinching sharply (8)
13 - Largely aquatic mammals (6)
14 - Assault (6)
15 - Respite (6)
17 - Dividing boundary (4)

Enter the letter in each circled cell in the order given below to reveal a themed answer:

13D	7E	1C	5E	11K	9F	2C	11D	13B	10I	3E	2G

92

Clue: Founded in 1636, what is the oldest institution of higher learning in the United States? (7,10)

Across

1 - Paper printout of data (4,4)
5 - Protective crust (4)
9 - Silk fabric (5)
10 - Public square (5)
11 - Misleading clue (3,7)
14 - Consent to receive (6)
15 - Having only magnitude (of a quantity) (6)
17 - Not alike (10)
20 - Snarl (5)
21 - Worthy principle or aim (5)
22 - Portion of medicine (4)
23 - Secondary personality (5,3)

Down

1 - Chickens (4)
2 - Speak in a wild way (4)
3 - Despicable (12)
4 - Waterproof garment (6)
6 - Collarbone (8)
7 - Bighead (8)
8 - Showing gratitude (12)
12 - Dressed a wound (8)
13 - Cutting instrument (8)
16 - Optical (6)
18 - Where you are now (4)
19 - Highest male voice (4)

Enter the letter in each circled cell in the order given below to reveal a themed answer:

10K	13F	7M	12I	2I	5J	13A	11G	5L	8C	8G	5H	11B	9D

8I	10I	1H

Clue: Who served as Vice President from 2001-9? (4,6)

Across

1 - Form of carbon (8)
5 - Flat circular plate (4)
8 - Deprive of weapons (5)
9 - Become less dark (7)
10 - Observed (7)
12 - Enunciating (7)
14 - Fish-eating birds of prey (7)
16 - Sport with arrows (7)
18 - Unlawful (7)
19 - Severe (5)
20 - Standard (4)
21 - Liberties (8)

Down

1 - Adhesive (4)
2 - Andre ___ : former US tennis player (6)
3 - Mortify (9)
4 - Covering a roof with thin slabs (6)
6 - Whole (6)
7 - Royal domains (8)
11 - Moderate (9)
12 - Calling (8)
13 - Of the eye (6)
14 - Type of shellfish (6)
15 - Old Portuguese coin (6)
17 - Opposite of more (4)

Enter the letter in each circled cell in the order given below to reveal a themed answer:

13J	11F	9C	1M	5K	1E	4A	3M	13I	9G

94

Clue: Which peace treaty of 1973 was signed to establish peace in Vietnam? (5,5,7)

Across

1 - Monetary unit of South Africa (4)
3 - Great difficulty (8)
9 - Large ocean (7)
10 - Pertaining to sound (5)
11 - Dispirited (12)
13 - Deforms (6)
15 - Pointed stake (6)
17 - Not excusable (12)
20 - ___ Sharapova: tennis player (5)
21 - Pays no attention to (7)
22 - Disbelieves (8)
23 - Stated (4)

Down

1 - Swiftness (8)
2 - Narrow stretches of land (5)
4 - Agreement (6)
5 - Doubting (12)
6 - Subject to persistent nagging (7)
7 - Stride; rate of moving (4)
8 - Loving (12)
12 - Accented (8)
14 - Internal organs (7)
16 - Selfish person (6)
18 - Bodily pouch or sac (5)
19 - Flightless birds (4)

Enter the letter in each circled cell in the order given below to reveal a themed answer:

4K	2M	1A	11G	6M	13D	5I	5F	6K	5K	2A	2G	6E	10G

11K	5A	13C

Clue: Which national health insurance program began in 1966 under the Social Security Administration? (8)

Across

1 - Separated; detached (8)
5 - Invoice (4)
9 - Short high-pitched tone (5)
10 - Principle laid down by an authority (5)
11 - Daughters of a monarch (10)
14 - Interruption or gap (6)
15 - Scattered about untidily (6)
17 - Officer who administers the law (10)
20 - Do without (5)
21 - Willow tree (5)
22 - Plunder; take illegally (4)
23 - Male riders (8)

Down

1 - Money that is owed (4)
2 - Perception (4)
3 - Consequence of an event (12)
4 - Flowing back (6)
6 - Absorbed (8)
7 - Secret affairs (8)
8 - Coming from outside (12)
12 - Disgraceful (8)
13 - Pouched mammal (8)
16 - Wall painting; mural (6)
18 - Steadfast (4)
19 - Outer coat of the seed of a grain (4)

Enter the letter in each circled cell in the order given below to reveal a themed answer:

3L	10G	8K	8I	12G	12M	13H	10A

96

Clue: Which US President launched the Great Society domestic programs to eliminate poverty and racial injustice? (6,1,7)

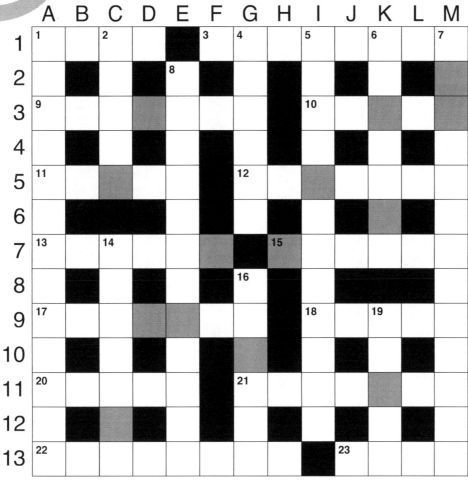

Across

1 - Vases (4)
3 - Shamefully bad (8)
9 - Release air from something (7)
10 - Cowboy display (5)
11 - Regal (5)
12 - Not strict (7)
13 - Violent atmospheric disturbances (6)
15 - Hold close (6)
17 - Chanted (7)
18 - Provide with necessary supplies (5)
20 - Concur (5)
21 - Tenth month of the year (7)
22 - Revealing a truth (8)
23 - Parched (4)

Down

1 - Make too low a guess (13)
2 - Attractively stylish (5)
4 - Very thin object used in sewing (6)
5 - Agreements; plans (12)
6 - Remnant (7)
7 - Easily angered (5-8)
8 - Accepted behavior whilst dining (5,7)
14 - The exposure of bedrock (7)
16 - Border; touch (6)
19 - Brown earth pigment (5)

Enter the letter in each circled cell in the order given below to reveal a themed answer:

3D	5C	7H	3K	9D	5I	11K	10G	3M	2M	9E	7F	12C	6K

Clue: In 1955, which African-American woman famously refused to give up her seat on a bus in Montgomery, Alabama? (4,5)

Across

1 - Garden flower (6)
4 - Late time of life (3,3)
9 - Inflatable rubber bag (7)
10 - Saturday and Sunday (7)
11 - ___ Hilfiger: US fashion designer (5)
12 - Stories (5)
14 - Dislikes intensely (5)
15 - Capital of Japan (5)
17 - Mythical monster (5)
18 - Social gathering with dancing (7)
20 - Game of chance (7)
21 - Badge of office (6)
22 - Be filled with love for (6)

Down

1 - Discussion (6)
2 - Distinctive feature (8)
3 - Form of sarcasm (5)
5 - Cries for (7)
6 - Fit of shivering (4)
7 - Discharges (6)
8 - Unintentionally (11)
13 - Oil-based flooring (8)
14 - Clutching (7)
15 - Fight (6)
16 - Sporting competitor (6)
17 - Person of exceptional importance (5)
19 - Writing fluids (4)

Enter the letter in each circled cell in the order given below to reveal a themed answer:

2E	1H	11A	4A	8M	1F	11L	12C	10A

98

Clue: Which leader founded the League of Women Voters and served as president of the National American Woman Suffrage Association? (6,7,4)

Across

1 - Scent (4)
3 - Lessening; diminishing (8)
9 - Cure-all (7)
10 - Barack ___ : former US President (5)
11 - Line segments in circles (5)
12 - Elusive (7)
13 - Make modern (6)
15 - Titaness in Greek mythology (6)
17 - Raging fire (7)
18 - Popular flowers (5)
20 - Inactive (5)
21 - Burst violently (7)
22 - Soak; drench (8)
23 - Snakelike fish (pl.) (4)

Down

1 - Chances for advancement (13)
2 - Possessed (5)
4 - Inclined at an angle (6)
5 - Therapeutic use of fragrances (12)
6 - Expect; conceive (7)
7 - Inelegance (13)
8 - Author of screenplays (12)
14 - Cause to deviate (7)
16 - An instant in time (6)
19 - Land along the edge of a sea (5)

Enter the letter in each circled cell in the order given below to reveal a themed answer:

12C	7D	9I	5A	5D	7F	3E	10K	13B	7B	10G	1F	9B	4M	3M	11E	7E

Clue: Which Spanish explorer led an expedition from Mexico to modern-day Kansas in 1540-2? (8)

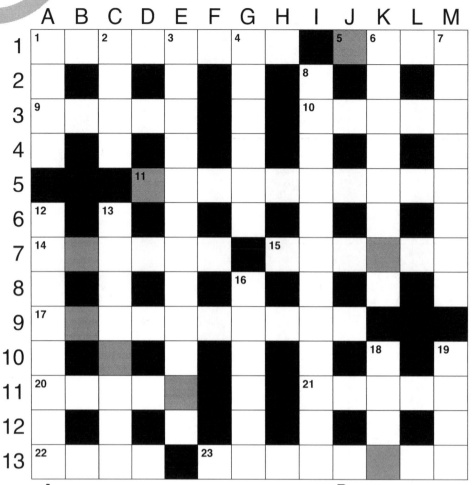

Across

1 - Power tool; buffer (8)
5 - Capital of Norway (4)
9 - Departing (5)
10 - Bring together (5)
11 - A decrease in loudness (10)
14 - Pay a casual visit to (4,2)
15 - Without delay (6)
17 - Fellow citizen (10)
20 - First tone of a scale (5)
21 - Heating apparatus (5)
22 - Light beams (4)
23 - Hairstyle (8)

Down

1 - Sheet of paper in a book (4)
2 - Put down (4)
3 - Importance (12)
4 - Panacea (6)
6 - Revolving quickly (8)
7 - Figure of speech (8)
8 - Mournfully (12)
12 - Teacher (8)
13 - Typically; usually (8)
16 - Cave (6)
18 - Cloud of gas around a comet (4)
19 - Become healthy again (4)

Enter the letter in each circled cell in the order given below to reveal a themed answer:

11E	9B	7B	10C	7K	13K	5D	1J

100

Clue: *Union general-in-chief Winfield Scott proposed which outline strategy for suppressing the Confederacy? (8,4)*

Across

1 - Curved shapes (4)
3 - Closed political meetings (8)
9 - Multiplied by three (7)
10 - Living in a city (5)
11 - Airing a TV program (12)
14 - Fruit of a rose (3)
16 - Sea duck (5)
17 - Bind (3)
18 - Extremely harmful; tragic (12)
21 - Small intestine (5)
22 - Domain (7)
23 - Extend beyond a surface (8)
24 - Rapid surprise attack (4)

Down

1 - German expressway (8)
2 - Doctrine; system of beliefs (5)
4 - Help (3)
5 - Musical technique (12)
6 - Fractional part (7)
7 - Of sound mind (4)
8 - Heavy long-handled tool (12)
12 - Detailed assessment of accounts (5)
13 - Greeted warmly (8)
15 - Inactive pill (7)
19 - Many-headed monster in Greek mythology (5)
20 - Walk awkwardly (4)
22 - Child (3)

Enter the letter in each circled cell in the order given below to reveal a themed answer:

9C	4I	3L	1F	13C	8A	13M	2M	7C	11B	13K	11I

1) THIRTEEN

2) NEW AMSTERDAM

3) MILLARD FILLMORE

4) THIRTEENTH

5) PHILADELPHIA

6) SEVEN SISTERS

7) PARIS

8) PROGRESSIVE

9) WINGS

10) PULLMAN STRIKE

11) IROQUOIS

12) TYLER

13) NEIL ARMSTRONG

14) TRUMAN DOCTRINE

15) CHANCELLORSVILLE

16) LOST GENERATION

17) JAMES DEAN

18) SOUTH DAKOTA

19) ZACHARY TAYLOR

20) MARILYN MONROE

21) GETTYSBURG

22) SPECTRAL

23) JANE ADDAMS

24) SYLVIA PLATH

25) GEORGE WASHINGTON

26) SPACE RACE

27) NATIONAL WOMAN'S PARTY

28) CORETTA SCOTT KING

29) FRANCIS SCOTT KEY

30) YORKTOWN

31) MANHATTAN PROJECT

32) JEFFERSON

33) JOE BIDEN

34) ROOSEVELT

35) STAUNTON

36) SILENT SENTINELS

37) CALVIN COOLIDGE

38) CALIFORNIA

39) ANNE BRADSTREET

40) NEW DEAL

41) COMMITTEE OF FIVE

42) MARGARET THATCHER

43) JIMMY CARTER

44) AL GORE

45) I HAVE A DREAM

46) HARLEM RENAISSANCE

47) AIN'T I A WOMAN?

48) JAMESTOWN

49) DONALD TRUMP

50) BETTY FRIEDAN

51) CAMDEN

52) PROHIBITION

53) LINDY HOP

54) HIRAM REVELS

55) MAYFLOWER

56) JEANNETTE RANKIN

57) RICHARD NIXON

58) MARSHALL PLAN

59) NEUTRALITY ACTS

60) GILDED AGE

61) LOUISA SWAIN

62) HARRY S. TRUMAN

63) HAWAII

64) FLAPPERS

65) ROANOKE COLONY

66) CHRYSLER BUILDING

67) MONROE DOCTRINE

68) BARACK OBAMA

69) FALL OF SAIGON

70) ABRAHAM LINCOLN

71) SALLY RIDE

72) UNCLE TOM'S CABIN

73) PULITZER PRIZE

74) BABE RUTH

75) BAY OF PIGS

76) ADAMS

77) ANDREW CARNEGIE

78) JOHN F. KENNEDY

79) LADY CHATTERLEY'S LOVER

80) GUADALUPE HIDALGO

81) MASSACHUSETTS

82) SPEAKEASY

83) RONALD REAGAN

84) ART DECO

85) FORT SUMTER

86) GROVER CLEVELAND

87) BOSTON TEA PARTY

88) DAN QUAYLE

89) KATY PERRY

90) MILHOUS

91) PALMITO RANCH

92) HARVARD UNIVERSITY

93) DICK CHENEY

94) PARIS PEACE ACCORDS

95) MEDICARE

96) LYNDON B. JOHNSON

97) ROSA PARKS

98) CARRIE CHAPMAN CATT

99) CORONADO

100) ANACONDA PLAN

...Solutions...

1.
```
P I L O T S _ O W _ S
A O _ M E D I A T O R
Y O U _ E D _ R L
O _ D U B L I N _ R U E D
F _ E _ T _ E _ A M
F A R A D _ A S I N I N E
_ L _ T _ S _ T
P I R A N H A _ H Y E N A
N _ C _ O T _ X _ P
A V E R _ U N W R A P _ O
O _ I _ G _ I _ E G G
S K E T C H E S _ C _ E
_ E _ Y _ T _ T A T T L E
```

2.
```
C A S T _ G R A F F I T I
A H D _ U R _ M _ D
N U R S I N G _ E X P E L
B U S _ E _ I _ Y
E M B A R R A S S I N G
R _ E R _ T _ G C
R E D _ P A S T A _ E V E
A R U _ O _ N _ N
_ S I T T I N G D U C K S
S B _ A _ I _ A U
K E B A B _ A W N I N G S
I L L _ D _ G D E
P R E T E N D S _ D Y E S
```

3.
```
B A S S _ C O N S I S T S
A T _ S _ R _ T _ A _ E
C A E S U R A _ R U M B A
K R P T A U S
H E N C E F O R W A R D
A R R B A H
N A M I N G _ M E R I N O
D O A A R P
_ P R O T U B E R A N C E
S T U A I L L
C H A I R _ C L E A N S E
A L A U S T S
R E S T L E S S _ W H Y S
```

4.

```
S O B S _ A D H E S I V E
E R M _ I X R F
L E A N I N G _ P R O O F
F V S I E N E
A L O F T _ T E R R I E R
S R S I N V
S I M M E R _ L E A G U E
U A A A N S
R E C I T E S _ T O P I C
A H M T I O E
N A I V E _ H O A R S E N
C N N M L E C
E V E N T U A L _ U R G E
```

5.
```
D E C A Y S _ C _ S _ B
E A _ C L U S T E R S
F L U _ U R A U
T _ G A M B I T _ R A T E
L H A A S A
Y E T I S _ S I G H T L Y
_ N P N I
R E A C T O R _ S P E C K
S R M S X R
E P E E _ P A T E N T _ O
R A O O _ R A N
M I S S O U R I _ A E
T E S _ C L O S E R
```

6.
```
V E A L _ C A P I T A L S
I D A C N R A
R E L A P S E _ S E T U P
I I P T D S
L A B O R A T O R I E S
I E E U C D
T E E _ C O M I C _ O D E
Y X I P T W
_ P A R A M I L I T A R Y
E M T O T E
C A P R I _ S E N S O R Y
H L O I S N E
O N E O N O N E _ L E N D
```

7.
```
C O Z Y _ O B E D I E N T
O E R E E A R
R O B B E R Y _ C U R I A
R R S O L N N
O V A T E _ N E A T E N S
B T D R S P
O R N A T E _ M A N T R A
R O L H T R
A U S T E R E _ I N U R E
T E M N O N N
I M B U E _ R I N G L E T
O A N Y S I L
N E G A T I V E _ S T A Y
```

8.

```
P O U N D I N G _ V E T O
A R E O H S P
W I D E N _ O U N T I E
S U O D M R N
_ A M A L G A M A T E
G G I E N N Y
L A R Y N X _ M I N G L E
A O A M T E D
C O U N T R Y M A N
I N I R R M B
A U D I O _ I M A G O
T E N A A G X
E D D Y _ I D E N T I T Y
```

9.

```
A L K A L I _ A B _ S
N U _ D E B I L I T Y
Y E N O Y U R
H _ G R I L L S _ B L I P
O F S S B K
W O U N D _ C A T E R E R
U B L R
T H O R E A U _ T Y P E S
O T B S O L
T U T U _ Y U C C A S
R R S U T I P
B L U E B I R D _ E U
Y D T _ S A T R A P
```

10.
```
A C U M E N _ R E S U M E
O I I E E R
B U R N _ P A L E N E S S
N A S I S
S T A R K _ B E D E V I L
D E O V N
C O S T E F F E C T I V E
W F D I O
E N M A S S E _ S M I L E
S H C P V
B A C K B O N E _ A X I S
I E O N N
C R E D I T _ T W I N G E
```

11.

```
P O R T A B L E _ A C I D
L A C I N H I
A P I S H _ M _ E X A M S
Y N I P W R P
_ R E C E P T A C L E
B I V T E O N
L I N K E D _ E S S A Y S
U E M S T L E
S E Q U E N T I A L
T U N R M M W
E D I C T _ O _ E X I L E
R T S N N T E
Y O Y O _ A G I T A T E D
```

12.

```
D U S K _ S P E C I O U S
E C I A O V A
S T R I N G S _ N E E D Y
P A C S S R S
A L P H A B E T I C A L
I N D D L P
R A P I D S _ K E P L E R
S R E D R E
_ C O N S E R V A T I S M
R R C I B V I
A B A T E _ F U L S O M E
S T N T Y R R
P H A N T A S M _ L Y R E
```

13.

14.

15.

16.

17.

18.

19.

20.

21.

22.

23.

24.

25.

A	S	P	S	■	P	R	I	M	R	O	S	E
P		A		M	E		A		R		X	
P	I	G	M	E	N	T	■	T	R	A	M	P
O		E		L		A		T		C		A
R	A	D	I	O	■	K	R	E	M	L	I	N
T			D		E	R		E		S		
I	G	N	O	R	E	■	B	O	N	S	A	I
O		O		A	I	F	■		V			
N	E	W	S	M	A	N	■	F	A	L	S	E
M		H		A		V		A		A		N
E	R	E	C	T	■	I	N	C	L	I	N	E
N		R		I		T		T		T		S
T	R	E	N	C	H	E	S	■	G	Y	M	S

26.

U	N	W	A	N	T	E	D	■	T	R	E	E
P		R		O		N		A		A		X
O	P	A	L	S	■	T	R	A	F	F	I	C
N		S		E		D		F		U		
■	S		S	D	■	I	T	A	L	I	C	S
S	P	E	C	I	A	L		N		A		I
T	E		V		X		X		N		N	
E	W	E	■	T	A	I	L	I	N	G		
A	B	R	I	D	G	E		O		N		
L		I		R		U		C		G		
I	N	T	E	G	E	R	■	S	L	I	D	E
N		E		O		L		T		L		
G	I	R	D	■	G	R	A	Y	N	E	S	S

27.

W	A	R	S	■	S	T	O	C	K	A	D	E
A		E		D	U		A		D		L	
R	E	S	T	I	N	G	■	P	U	M	P	S
R		E		S		I		I		E		
I	N	T	R	O	D	U	C	T	O	R	Y	■
O			B		N		A		E		S	
R	I	P	■	E	X	C	E	L	■	S	O	W
S		L		D		L		I		E		
■	B	U	S	I	N	E	S	S	L	I	K	E
C		M		E		T		N		T		
A	G	A	I	N	■	D	W	I	N	D	L	E
R		G		C		R		C		E		S
P	R	E	C	E	D	E	D	■	E	X	I	T

28.

T	O	L	L	■	E	C	L	I	P	S	E	S
R		O		M	A		N		O		H	
A	X	O	L	O	T	L	■	C	E	L	L	O
N		K		T		L		O		V		O
S	U	S	H	I	■	E	E	R	I	E	S	T
P			V		D		P		N			I
O	U	T	L	A	Y	■	C	O	T	T	O	N
S		Y		T		E		R				G
I	M	P	L	I	E	D	■	A	M	I	S	S
T		I		O		I		T		N		T
I	B	S	E	N	■	S	P	E	C	T	R	A
O		T		A		O		D		R		R
N	E	S	T	L	I	N	G	■	B	O	W	S

29.

U	N	M	A	S	K	■	T	E	A	C	U	P
N		Y		H		R		F		L		A
R	E	S	U	R	G	E	■	F	U	R		R
U		T		U	■	G	O	O	D	B	Y	E
L	Y	I	N	G		R		R		N		
Y		C		E	■	T	R	U	S	T		
■		A	■	N	O	T	E	S		N		
S	A	L	S	A		T			W	N		
U				T		A	■	M	O	O	S	E
D	I	S	T	U	R	B		A		R		E
D		W		R		A		E		A		H
E	A	A		E		A		E		A	H	E
N	I	B	B	L	E	■	S	W	A	Y	E	D

30.

S	T	A	R	S	I	G	N	■	M	Y	T	H
E		N		E		R		B	E		E	
E	X	T	O	L	■	O		L	L	A	M	A
D		I		F		U		A		R		V
■		■	D	E	S	P	I	C	A	B	L	Y
B		B		M		S		K		O		S
A	B	R	U	P	T	■	P	A	R	O	L	E
T		O		L		D		N		K		T
H	O	W	D	O	Y	O	U	D	O	■		
R		B		Y		M		B		T		H
O	B	E	S	E		I		L	E	A	S	E
O		A		D		N		U		X		L
M	A	T	H	■	S	O	L	E	C	I	S	M

31.

I	N	C	U	R	S	■	U	S	E	F	U	L
D		O		A		L		I		L		I
I	G	N	O	B	L	E	■	R	E	V		V
O		C		I		V	I	O	L	A	T	E
C	R	E	E	D	■	E		C		L		L
Y		R		L		L	C	A	R	R	Y	
■		T		Y	A	H	O	O		E		
U	N	I	T	E		E		C		C		C
N		L		A		P	O	K	E	R		U
J	U	M	B	L	E	D		E		L		U
U		O		I		E	N	D	L	E	S	S
S		N		N		D		A		S		T
T	H	O	U	G	H	■	G	L	O	S	S	Y

32.

H	E	A	R	■	F	R	U	I	T	F	U	L
A		S		D		Y		N		A		O
R	E	P	T	I	L	E	■	V	O	T	E	S
D		I		V		■		U		I		E
B	A	C	T	E	R	I	O	L	O	G	Y	
A		R		N		N		N		U		C
C	U	E	■	S	O	L	V	E	■	E	R	A
K			J	I		A		R		S		S
■	A	E	R	O	D	Y	N	A	M	I	C	S
G		C		N		B		S		E		E
E	X	T	R	A	■	V	A	L	I	A	N	T
M		O		R		A		E		A		T
S	P	R	A	Y	I	N	G	■	A	C	R	E

33.

L	O	A	T	H	E	■	S	H	A	G	G	Y
U		S		E		H		A		R		O
C	A	S	C	A	D	E	■	R	U	D		D
E		O		T		L	O	V	A	B	L	E
N	O	R	M	S		I		E		L		L
T		T		C		S	T	A	R	S		
■		E		■	F	L	O	U	T	■	P	
U	N	D	U	E		P		T		T		S
G				G		E		T	■	H	O	I	S	T
A	D	J	U	D	G	E		U		T		A
N		U		I		R	E	S	C	U	E	S
D		G		N		S		K		D		
A	S	S	I	G	N	■	A	S	S	E	T	S

34.

R	I	T	E	■	R	E	S	P	O	N	S	E
A		R		N		C		H		O		A
T	R	I	V	I	A	L	■	I	R	O	N	S
I		E		G		A		L		D		E
F	O	R	T	H	R	I	G	H	T	L	Y	■
I			T		R		A		E			S
E	N	T	I	C	E	■	F	R	O	S	T	Y
D		A		L		S		M				N
■		U	N	C	O	N	T	R	O	L	L	E	D
S		K		T		R		N		O		R
T	E	E	T	H	■	O	R	I	N	O	C	O
U		R		E		D		C		S		M
D	I	S	A	S	T	E	R	■	G	E	N	E

35.

B	A	C	K	E	D	■	I	■	A	■	S	
Y		O		■	R	E	S	O	N	A	T	E
P	U	P		A		O		D		R		
L		P	R	I	M	A	L	■	R	E	E	L
A		E		A		A		O		S		
Y	A	R	D	S	■	A	T	H	I	R	S	T
■			I		P		E		D			
S	C	R	A	P	E	D	■	P	S	A	L	M
	O		M		N		B			M		E
E	U	R	O	■	S	C	A	M	P	I	■	R
	G		N		I		R			D	I	G
H	A	N	D	B	O	O	K	■	S			E
	R			S		N	■	S	U	I	T	E	D

36.

D	E	B	A	R	K	■	B	E	D	L	A	M
E		L		I		C		X		A		O
D	E	A	D	S	E	A	■	H		N		U
U		S		E		N	E	A	T	E	S	T
C	I	T	E	S		D		U				H
E		O		■		L		S	I	T	E	S
■			F		S	C	E	N	T	■	R	
B	E	F	I	T		P			A		P	
R			O		O		R	A	V	E	R	
O	U	T	G	R	O	W		E		E	I	
O		A		A		E	N	S	U	R	E	D
C		N		G		R		T		S		
H	O	S	T	E	L	■	U	S	H	E	R	S

37.
```
N O S T R I L S . L I M B
A . T . A . A . N . . U
M A O R I . Y O U N G E R
E . R . N . O . . E . G
. . E W . U T E N S I L
R E D R A F T . N . T . A
E . . T . . . H . . . R
L . A E . G L A N C E S
E N F O R C E . N . A . .
A . R . N . C . N . R
S W I N D L E . I T C H Y
E . C . V . N . E . A
D E A R . P A N G O L I N
```

38.
```
P A D S . E Y E P I E C E
E . I . A . E . R . V . A
R E C A S T S . O B O E S
S . E . T . V . L . . T
U N D E R A C H I E V E
A . . O . O D E . . E F
D E W . P U R G E . S K I
E . E . H . G . N . . R
. L A B Y R I N T H I N E
. C . R . S . I . N . W
H A I T I . B R A V A D O
A . E . C . A . L . N O
R E D E S I G N . L E A D
```

39.
```
W E R E W O L F . I D E A
E . O . A . E . . O . N
L I C I T . A I L E R O N
T . O . E . V . S . . O
. . C . R . . E S T U A R Y
P R O F F E R . R . L . I
A . . . A . A . N
L . E L . P O U R I N G
P E D D L E R . M . R . T
A . B . . A . A . O . T
B R E W E R Y . T E N T H
L . R . . E . I . E . U
E D G Y . P R E C E D E S
```

40.
```
A N A R C H I C . U S E D
N . D . O . M . A . E . I
T W A I N . B . M E A L S
S . M . F . I . A . R . A
. . D I A B O L I C A L
R . W . R . E . G . H . L
E N I G M A . G A Z E B O
V . N . A . B . M . D . W
A D D I T I O N A L
M . F . I . D . T . A . V
P I A N O . I . I S S U E
E . L . N . L . O . K . T
D O L L . H Y P N O S I S
```

41.
```
O I L S . M A L A Y S I A
V . O . D . R . D . U . C
E G O T I S T . D E P O T
R . M . F . I . P . S
D I S A F F E C T I O N
R . I . A . I . S . C
A G A . C A R G O . E T A
W . T . U . T . N . N
. W H O L E H E A R T E D
I . E . T . . L . O . I
C H I L I . A L L O W E D
E . S . E . L . Y . E . L
D O M E S T I C . T R A Y
```

42.
```
C O C O . S P A C E M A N
O . O . F . U . H . O . E
M O N S O O N . A U R A L
P . G . R . I . M . D . S
R E A R M . S O P R A N O
E . . A . H . I . N . N
H A S S L E . B O T T O M
E . A . D . A . N . . A
N A T T E R S . S P A I N
S . I . H . S . H . D . D
I T A L Y . I M I T A T E
V . T . D . S . P . P . L
E X E G E T I C . E T N A
```

43.
```
L I K E N E S S . O M A R
I . E . E . T . A . . E
L Y R I C . I N V O K E D
Y . N . E . G . . E . I
. . E . S . M E A N D E R
M E L I S S A . P . O . E
O . . A . . O . . . C
L . A R . A C C O U N T
A S S A Y E D . R . P
S . S . . J . Y . R . B
S H I A T S U . P R O W L
E . S . . R . H . O . O
S I T S . S E M A N T I C
```

44.
```
N O A H . V I A D U C T S
E . S . I . O . I . A . L
A L S O R A N . C A N D O
R . E . R . . T . T . G
M A T H E M A T I C A L
I . V . L . O . T . U
S E C . E A T E N . A W N
S . O . R . O . A . . S
. I M M E A S U R A B L E
M . P . N . . I . L . T
A D U L T . P R E S E N T
K . T . L . E . S . N . L
E V E R Y O N E . E D G E
```

45.
```
A P E S . H A B I T A T S
N . L . B . D . N . G . E
T U T O R E D . F E A S T
E . O . E . L . E . I . S
C O N V A L E S C E N T
E . . S . D . T . S . I
D A I N T Y . L I S T E N
E . T . S . A . O . . V
. H A U T E C O U T U R E
M . L . R . T . S . R . R
A M I G O . O B L I G E S
R . A . K . R . Y . E . E
C A N O E I S T . O D D S
```

46.
```
C L I M A T I C . P A L L
U . B . B . B . P . D . U
P I E R S . E . E T H I C
S . X . E . R . R . E . I
. . I N D I S P O S E D
E . E T . A . E . I . I
M A X I M S . U T M O S T
O . E . I . M . U . N . Y
T Y R A N N I C A L
I . T . D . L . T . W . E
O L I V E . A . I N A P T
N . O . D . N . O . I . C
S E N T . T O P N O T C H
```

47.
```
N E R O . W H I S P E R S
O . A . B . A . E . A . L
T U R K E Y S . L A R G E
E . E . L . . F . D . D
B U R G L A R A L A R M
O . . I . O . E . U . S
O R C . G L U E S . M O P
K . H . E . G . S . . E
. R E P R E H E N S I O N
A . V . E . . E . D . D
R E R U N . S A S H I M I
C . O . C . H . S . O . N
H O N E Y B E E . S T A G
```

48.
```
E N M I T Y . S C A R A B
X . A . R . P . O . A . L
T E R M I N I . N . C . A
E . K . A . E S C H E W S
N A D A L . I . O . . T
D . O . N . . R O C K S
. . W . A C T E D . O
F E N D S . H . . N . M
A . . T . E . M A C R O
R I B B O N S . E . R . U
O . R . U . K I D N E Y S
F . I . N . Y . I . T . S
F J O R D S . S C H E M E
```

49.
```
RUTS.ATTENDED
E.R.C.O.F.E.I
AGITATE.FUMES
S.L.P...O.E.H
SELFINTEREST.
E...T.O.T.N.E
SAP.USUAL.ELF
S.R.L.C.E...F
.METAPHYSICAL
S.V.T...S.L.U
KHAKI.PILLAGE
U.I.O.H.Y.M.N
ATLANTIC.SPAT
```

50.
```
BRANCH.HORDES
.E.E.O.E.I.W
DIVA.SIDESTEP
.T.R.T.O.E
SEWED.ENCRYPT
.R.S.G.I...O
FAITHLESSNESS
.T...O.M.E.S
DENMARK.EGGED
..A.I.Y.A.S
WELLTODO.TOSS
.F.T.U.G.E.E
STRAWS.INSIDE
```

51.
```
TAPE.COMPOSER
H.A.T.D.Y.E.E
RETIRED.REALM
E.I.A.S.O.F.O
ACORN.OUTMOST
T...S.N.E.O.E
EFFACE.ACIDIC
N.A.E.I.H...O
INTENDS.NOLIN
N.E.D.S.I.O.T
GAFFE.UNCOVER
L.U.N.E.S.E.O
YULETIDE.IDOL
```

52.
```
SHATTERS.MALI
O.U.E.E...C.N
DURUM.HYDRANT
A.O.P.A...C.R
.R.L.SUFFICE
PHARAOH.I.A.P
A.T...N...N.I
T.M.E.HAGGLED
THIRSTY.E.A.S
E.S...B.R.Z.S
RATTLER.THUMP
N.E...I.I.L.U
SIRE.ADOPTION
```

53.
```
ANATHEMA.KIEV
C.P.E.A.F.L.I
HOSTA.ELLEN
Y.E.R.U.A.T.E
..STIRFRYING
A.I.R.E.L.M.A
MEMBER.METEOR
I.M.N.B.S.D.Y
CLOUDBURST
A.R.I.S.N.Y.S
BATON.EXULT
L.A.G.E.S.A.I
ELLS.PRISONER
```

54.
```
SMUDGE.TULIPS
.E.R.Y.R.A.R
SAGA.ELECTRON
.N.S.D.S.I
SWATS.STANDBY
.H.I.L.L.R
CIRCUMVENTION
.L...M.S.R.A
PELICAN.SAUDI
..M.N.S.N.C
SHIPMENT.CIAO
.E.E.N.E.H.S
ANKLET.PRETTY
```

55.
```
MOCK.THRILLED
E.H.W.U.N.A.I
TRAVELS.CAMPS
E.F.L.H.O.B.A
OFFAL.UNHEARD
R...I.P.E.D.V
OCEANS.ARMADA
L.L.F.M.E...N
ORATORY.NIGHT
G.T.R.O.T.L.A
IDIOM.PULLING
S.O.E.I.Y.D.G
TONEDEAF.FEED
```

56.
```
DEFIES.A.D.A
E.O...PICKINGS
JAR.R.Q.R.R
E.MILIEU.EVEN
C.A.G.I.C.E
TITLE.PROTEST
..A.B.E.E
SCANDAL.ADEPT
.H.G.H.V.N.U
TOFU.REEKED.N
.R.A.A.R.EYE
JUGGLING.A.U
.S.E.N.ENTRAP
```

57.
```
OVERPLAY.LARA
U.X.L.B...D.N
ZAIRE.OUTRAGE
O.T.N.A.P.C
.E.T.RELATED
MUDDIED.O.S.O
A...F.U...T
R.E.U.PRIMATE
REGALLY.S.N
I.O.T.I.T.A
AZIMUTH.ALLOW
G.S...O.N.E
EMMY.UNFAIRLY
```

58.
```
HOSTELRY.CLAP
O.I.X.O.M.E.A
WATCH.N.OCCUR
L.E.I.D.T.T.O
..BLOODHOUND
B.P.A.S.E.R.I
ERRORS.BREEZE
S.E.A.A.T.D.S
MEDITATION.
I.A.I.T.N.L.P
RETRO.A.GUANO
C.O.N.C.U.U.N
HERB.SHEEPDOG
```

59.
```
SEWN.PROMISED
T.O.I.E.U.E
ALMANAC.AUNTS
C.A.T.I.S.B.K
CONTEMPTUOUS
A...R.E.R.R.P
TARIFF.LEANTO
O.E.E.B.M.L
.USERFRIENDLY
S.E.E.I.N.E.G
CANON.DUTIFUL
U.T.C.E.S.E.O
DISPERSE.BRAT
```

60.
```
THRESHED.HELP
E.E.C.R.D.X.R
ELDER.A.IMAGE
S.O.E.S.S.M.C
..BENEFICIAL
R.A.N.R.N.N.U
ALLOWS.AGREED
M.L.R.I.E.D.E
PHILISTINE.
A.A.T.A.U.Y.S
RANGE.L.OVERT
T.C.R.I.U.T.U
STEW.SCISSION
```

61.

M	O	T	E			S	E	N	T	I	E	N	T
A		R		P		N		O		N			R
G	O	A	H	E	A	D		G	U	A	V	A	
N		I		R		I	E		E	M			N
I	D	L	E	S			N	U	T	M	E	G	S
F				I		G		H		L			C
I	N	S	I	S	T		L	E	S	S	E	E	
C		W		T		A		R					N
A	Z	A	L	E	A	S		N	A	M	E	D	
T		L		N		P		E		A			E
I	N	L	E	T			I	N	S	U	L	I	N
O		O		L		R			S			L	C
N	E	W	L	Y	W	E	D			I	S	L	E

62.

E	L	L	E			E	T	H	I	O	P	I	A
N		I		M		I		M		R		X	
C	A	P	T	I	O	N		P	H	O	T	O	
L		I		S			R		V			N	
O	L	D	F	A	S	H	I	O	N	E	D		
S				D		A		V		R		W	
E	A	T		V	A	L	U	E		B	O	O	
S		E		E		L		M				N	
	U	N	I	N	T	E	R	E	S	T	E	D	
S		S		T			N		U			E	
H	A	I	K	U		T	I	T	U	L	A	R	
U		O		R			S		I			I	E
T	E	N	D	E	N	C	Y			S	P	E	D

63.

D	E	A	L			N	O	B	O	D	I	E	S
O		D		I		D		V		N			U
W	I	D	E	N	E	D		E	A	T	E	R	
N		L		C		I		R		R			F
P	R	E	P	O	S	T	E	R	O	U	S		
O				M		Y		E		D			S
U	S	U	R	P	S		C	A	R	E	E	R	
R		N		A		F		C					I
	M	U	L	T	I	L	A	T	E	R	A	L	
S		S		I		E		I		A			A
T	H	U	M	B		D	O	O	R	M	E	N	
A		A		L		G		N		P			K
B	E	L	I	E	V	E	S			A	S	I	A

64.

65.

R	A	S	H	E	S		C		A		S	
I		U				O	V	E	R	T	A	K	E
O	F	F		G		N		T		E		
T		F	O	R	G	E	S		I	N	T	O
E		E		Y		U		T		C		
R	U	R	A	L		B	R	O	U	G	H	T
			C	N		E		D				
P	A	T	C	H	E	S		N	E	S	T	S
	L		E	M		A		T				E
C	L	I	P		E	N	D	U	R	E		E
	E		T		S	A				R	A	M
A	G	R	E	E	I	N	G			E		L
	E		D		S		E	M	B	O	D	Y

66.

S	A	L	T			N	A	R	R	A	T	E	S
K		I		F		R		E		H			U
E	N	L	A	R	G	E		P	L	I	E	D	
L		A		E			E		N			S	
E	X	C	R	U	C	I	A	T	I	N	G		
T				D		M		I		E			R
A	F	T		I	N	P	U	T		R	U	E	
L		E		A		L		I					W
	P	E	N	N	S	Y	L	V	A	N	I	A	
S		M		S			E		E			I	R
T	W	I	L	L		O	B	L	I	G	E	D	
U		N		I		W		Y		Y		E	E
B	I	G	A	P	P	L	E			T	R	O	D

67.

68.

M	U	C	K			F	A	R	C	I	C	A	L
A		O		S		P		O		O			A
C	A	P	T	U	R	E		N	I	P	P	Y	
H		S		R			V		Y			S	
I	N	E	X	P	E	R	I	E	N	C	E		
S				R		O		N		A			B
M	A	T		I	N	G	O	T		T	A	U	
O		U		S		U		I					O
	P	R	A	I	S	E	W	O	R	T	H	Y	
B		M		N			N		H				A
A	L	O	N	G		T	R	A	D	E	I	N	
L		I		L		E		L		M			C
M	I	L	K	Y	W	A	Y			R	E	L	Y

69.

S	I	E	R	R	A			P		U		M	
A		L				G	E	R	A	N	I	U	M
V	I	A		A		E		H		S			
A		G	S			E	U		R			I	
E	V	E	N	T		A	D	A	M	A	N	T	
			E		P		E		E				
S	H	O	W	M	A	N		E	D	I	F	Y	
E		S		Y		M				C			A
T	A	L	C		M	U	E	S	L	I			W
	T		A		E		D				C	A	N
H	E	L	S	I	N	K	I			L			E
	D		T		T			A	F	I	E	L	D

70.

71.

D	R	E	D	G	E			X	E	R	X	E	S
E		P		A		S		N		M			P
S	T	I	M	U	L	I		E		E			E
I		D		G		N	O	M	I	N	A	L	
S	I	E	G	E		G		I					L
T		M				U		E	X	I	T	S	
		I		T	I	L	T	S				N	
C	A	C	A	O		A				V			P
I		K		R			S	H	E	E	R		
T	S	U	N	A	M	I		I			S		A
R		M			T	I	G	H	T	L	Y		
I		I		D		A		Y		H		O	E
C	L	O	C	K	S			S	T	A	R	E	D

72.

...Solutions...

73.
```
C A P S   J U N K M A I L
R   I   I   N   A   P   A
E X P A N D S   L A P A Z
D   I   F   E   E   A   Y
I N T E R M E D I A R Y
T       I   N   D   E   G
O O Z I N G   H O W L E R
R   A   G   O   S       E
  I M P E R F E C T I O N
O   B   M   F   O   C   A
W H E R E   E M P T I E D
E   Z   N   R   E   L   E
S K I T T I S H   E Y E S
```

74.
```
S I E N N A   E   P   A
C   L     B A S E L E S S
A N A   O   T   A   T
R   T R I V I A   C O R E
C   E   E   E   T   A   A
E N D O W   B E T R A Y S
      N   E   S   D
D E S C E N T   O S C A R
  M   O   G   F   A   O
F I L M   U N I T E S   U
  G   I   L   E     K E N
T R A N S F E R   E   D
  E   G   S   Y O U T H S
```

75.
```
D R I P   A D V A N C E S
A   G   I   I   C   A   E
T A L E N T S   K A R M A
A   O   D   O   N   R   N
B O O G I E W O O G I E
A     S   N   W   E   P
S H O U T S   P L U R A L
E   B   I   F   E     A
  E V E N H A N D E D L Y
A   I   C   M   G   R   R
C L O U T   O R E G A N O
H   L   U   D   F O
E S S A Y I S T   A T O M
```

76.
```
C A F E   P E N U M B R A
O   O   C   R   N   U   C
M A R S H E S   C O N I C
P   A   E   A   H   C   I
R H Y M E   T R A S H E D
E     S   Z   R   E   E
H A S T E N   H I D D E N
E   O   B   D   T     T
N E P T U N E   A E S O P
S   H   R   P   B   I   R
I C I N G   A L L E G R O
O   S   E   R   E   N   N
N U M E R A T E   A S H E
```

77.
```
D O G H O U S E   C H I C
E   A   R   H   A   A
F E I G N   R E M A R K S
T   N   A   U   R   T
  E M   G O N D O L A
L I D L E S S   E   W   N
I     I   N   U   E
T W T   E A R S H O T
T R E S S E D   A   A
O   A     G   L   W   H
R A V I O L I   G R A V Y
A   E     L   I   I   P
L A D S   D Y N A M I T E
```

78.
```
B O D I C E   A S Y L U M
E   I   R   N   A   I   A
R E L E A S E   M   V   S
E   I   Z   C Y P R E S S
F O G G Y   E   R     E
T   E     S   A C H E S
  N   R I S K S   E
H I T C H   A   I   E
I     I   R   V E G A N
J A C U Z Z I   A   H   Z
A   O   O   L I G H T L Y
C   G   M   Y   U   E   M
K I S S E D   S E A N C E
```

79.
```
L O S S   M N E M O N I C
U   H   U   U   U   E   R
C H I G N O N   L A S S O
K   F   P   C   T   T   P
I N T E L L I G I B L Y
E     E   O   L   E   C
S O C I A L   W I L D E R
T   E   S   S   N     U
  A D V A N T A G E O U S
O   I   N   A   U   U   A
P I L O T   D R A I N E D
A   L   L   I   L   C   E
L E A P Y E A R   H E I R
```

80.
```
C O N S E R V E   A D D S
U   O   S   A   R   E
T E N E T   L   S T O R M
S   R   C   T   P   E
    P A R A G R A P H S
E   N   N   O   I   T
M A N A G E   G L A N C E
I   T   E   B   O   G   R
S E I S M O L O G Y
S   C   E   O   I   S   B
A L I E N   W   C R E P E
R   N   T   U   A   M   R
Y O G A   A P P L Y I N G
```

81.
```
B U S T   E N C I R C L E
E   C   R   E   N   A   A
S L O W E S T   C R Y P T
T   R   M     O   E   S
R E N O U N C E M E N T
I     N   L   P   N   N
D O T   E R A S E   E K E
E   W   R   S   T     E
  M I S A P P R E H E N D
M   N   T     N   P   L
E N N U I   S U C R O S E
S   E   V   E   Y   C   S
S A D D E N E D   O H M S
```

82.
```
C O M E D Y   B A C K E R
A   A   I   F   P   N   E
S T I N G E R   R   O   N
U   N   I   A D O P T E D
A L L O T   G   P     E
L   A     M   O R D E R
  N   D R E G S   E
W E D G E   N     S   F
A     L   T   G L O B E
R E P L I C A   I   L   A
M   E   G   R E V E A L S
U   A   H   Y   E   T   T
P E T I T E   A N G E L S
```

83.
```
P O U T   G A M B L E R S
R   N   D   T   I   D   U
O F F B E A T   B L I M P
G   I   M   A   L   F   P
R A T I O   I N I T I A L
E     N   N   O   C   E
S P A R S E   A G L E A M
S   D   T   A   R     E
I N V E R T S   A S H E N
V   E   A   T   P   I   T
E G R E T   E C H I D N A
L   S   R   Y   E   R
Y I E L D I N G   E S P Y
```

84.
```
E V A D E D   V O L U M E
  O   E   U   E   O   A
S C A N   P A S S W O R D
  A   T   E   U   E
S T R I P   A V E R A G E
I   S   D   I     O
C O N T R I B U T I O N S
N     S   S   M   D
E S C O R T S   S P O O K
  D   R   T   O   L
U N L I K E L Y   U N I T
O   U   S   P   N   E
C R U M B S   E L D E R S
```

85.
S	A	H	A	R	A		E		A		M	
C		I			S	I	N	I	S	T	E	R
H	I	S		T		V		T		T		
O		S	L	E	E	P	Y		E	A	R	N
O		E		R		I		R		I		I
L	A	S	T	S		U	N	H	I	T	C	H
		E		C		G		S				
C	R	E	A	T	O	R		S	K	I	E	S
	U		S		N		I		N		T	
N	E	A	P		C	A	N	D	I	D		E
	F		O		E		L			U	M	A
A	U	T	O	M	A	T	A		C		M	
	L		N		L		W	I	N	T	R	Y

86.
V	E	R	T	I	C	A	L		K	E	L	P
A		E		N		R			L		L	
I	D	L	E	D		O	V	E	R	U	S	E
N		A		I		U			D		A	
	T		C		S	Y	S	T	E	M	S	
P	R	E	L	A	T	E		U		D		U
R			T				B			R		R
O		O		E		T	A	D	P	O	L	E
V	A	N	E	S	S	A		I		G		U
I		E				I		V		R		U
D	O	O	R	M	A	N		I	D	E	A	S
E		F				T		D		S		E
S	A	F	E		A	S	S	E	S	S	O	R

87.
M	O	R	I	B	U	N	D		E	R	O	S
E		I		I			A		A		E	
M	A	N	G	O		C		N	O	D	E	S
O		D		C		E		T		O		P
			W	H	I	T	E	H	O	U	S	E
E		P		E		Y		R		B		N
S	H	R	I	M	P		F	O	O	L	E	D
C		O		I		G		P		E		S
A	M	B	A	S	S	A	D	O	R			
L		A		T		T		L		S		F
A	M	B	E	R		E		O	T	T	E	R
T		L		Y		A		G		A		E
E	V	E	S		D	U	T	Y	F	R	E	E

88.
O	B	O	E		A	C	A	D	E	M	I	C
B		P		A		R		I		A		A
S	T	E	E	P	L	E		S	I	R	E	N
I		R		P		A		S		T		E
D	I	A	G	R	A	M	M	A	T	I	C	
I		E		Y		T		N		N		B
A	L	I	G	H	T		B	I	K	I	N	I
N		C		E		U		S				C
	M	E	A	N	I	N	G	F	U	L	L	Y
L		P		S		C		I		O		C
A	L	I	B	I		U	N	E	Q	U	A	L
I		C		O		R		D		S		E
R	E	K	I	N	D	L	E		B	Y	E	S

89.
H	O	M	E	W	O	R	K		W	I	F	I
A		A		A		E			M		D	
C	A	D	E	T		G	L	I	M	P	S	E
K		D		E		R		U		A		A
	E		R		I	L	L	E	G	A	L	
K	I	N	G	P	I	N		A		N		I
E				O		B						Z
Y		O	L		A	N	Y	T	I	M	E	
H	A	P	L	O	I	D		R		N		
O		E			V		I		B		I	
L	I	N	K	A	G	E		N	O	O	K	S
E		E			N		T		R		R	
S	A	R	I		E	T	C	H	I	N	G	S

90.
S	I	D	E		F	R	A	C	T	U	R	E
E		A		P		A		L		N		V
L	I	Z	A	R	D	S		E	V	A	D	E
F		E		I		C		A		W		R
C	E	D	E	D		A	I	R	M	A	I	L
O				E		L		S		R		A
N	O	S	H	O	W		R	I	D	E	R	S
F		P		F		D		G				T
E	C	L	I	P	S	E		H	A	N	O	I
S		U		L		N		T		O		N
S	Y	R	I	A		O	P	E	N	I	N	G
E		G		C		T		D		S		L
D	E	E	P	E	N	E	D		D	E	W	Y

91.
S	O	L	V	E	N	T	S		A	G	E	S
O		O		N		H			U		P	
R	E	L	I	C		R	I	S	O	T	T	O
T		L		O		O			T		N	
	O		M		W	O	N	D	E	R	S	
T	O	P	S	P	I	N		U		R		O
W		A				I		I				R
E		O	S		A	S	S	U	R	E	S	
A	R	T	I	S	T	S		A		E		
K		T			S		N		L		W	
I	N	E	R	T	I	A		C	H	I	N	A
N		R			E		E		E		A	
G	A	S	P		B	L	I	S	S	F	U	L

92.
H	A	R	D	C	O	P	Y		S	C	A	B
E		A		O		O		A		L		R
N	I	N	O	N		N		P	L	A	Z	A
S		T		T		C		P		V		G
			R	E	D	H	E	R	R	I	N	G
B		S		M		O		E		C		A
A	C	C	E	P	T		S	C	A	L	A	R
N		I		T		V		I		E		T
D	I	S	S	I	M	I	L	A	R			
A		S		B		S		T		H		A
G	R	O	W	L		U		I	D	E	A	L
E		R		E		A		V		R		T
D	O	S	E		A	L	T	E	R	E	G	O

93.
G	R	A	P	H	I	T	E		D	I	S	K
L		G		U		I			N		I	
U	N	A	R	M		L	I	G	H	T	E	N
E		S		I		I		A		G		
	S		L		N	O	T	I	C	E	D	
V	O	I	C	I	N	G		E		T		O
O				A		A		M				M
C		O	T		O	S	P	R	E	Y	S	
A	R	C	H	E	R	Y		E		S		
T		U			S		R		C		L	
I	L	L	I	C	I	T		A	C	U	T	E
O		A			E		T		D		S	
N	O	R	M		F	R	E	E	D	O	M	S

94.
R	A	N	D		H	A	R	D	S	H	I	P
A		E		A		C		I		E		A
P	A	C	I	F	I	C		S	O	N	I	C
I		K		F		O		B		P		E
D	I	S	H	E	A	R	T	E	N	E	D	
I				C		D		L		C		S
T	W	I	S	T	S		P	I	C	K	E	T
Y		N		I		E		E				R
	U	N	F	O	R	G	I	V	A	B	L	E
E		A		N		O		I		U		S
M	A	R	I	A		I	G	N	O	R	E	S
U		D		T		S		G		S		E
S	U	S	P	E	C	T	S		S	A	I	D

95.
D	I	V	O	R	C	E	D		B	I	L	L
E		I		E		B		A		N		I
B	L	E	E	P		B		D	O	G	M	A
T		W		E		I		V		E		I
			P	R	I	N	C	E	S	S	E	S
S		K		C		G		N		T		O
H	I	A	T	U	S		S	T	R	E	W	N
A		N		S		F		I		D		S
M	A	G	I	S	T	R	A	T	E			
E		A		I		E		I		F		B
F	O	R	G	O		S		O	S	I	E	R
U		O		N		C		U		R		A
L	O	O	T		H	O	R	S	E	M	E	N

96.
U	R	N	S		I	N	F	A	M	O	U	S
N		I		T		E		R		D		H
D	E	F	L	A	T	E		R	O	D	E	O
E		T		B		D		A		M		R
R	O	Y	A	L		L	E	N	I	E	N	T
E				E		E		G		N		T
S	T	O	R	M	S		N	E	S	T	L	E
T		U		A		M						M
I	N	T	O	N	E	D		E	Q	U	I	P
M		C		N		J		N		M		E
A	G	R	E	E		O	C	T	O	B	E	R
T		O			I		S		E		E	
E	X	P	O	S	I	N	G		A	R	I	D

...Solutions...

97.

D	A	H	L	I	A		O	L	D	A	G	E
E		A		R		U		A		G		X
B	A	L	L	O	O	N		M		U		U
A		L		N		W	E	E	K	E	N	D
T	O	M	M	Y		I		N				E
E		A		R		T		T	A	L	E	S
		R		H	A	T	E	S		I		
T	O	K	Y	O		I			N		P	
U			L		N		T	R	O	L	L	
S	H	I	N	D	I	G		I		L		A
S		N		I		L	O	T	T	E	R	Y
L		K		N		Y		A		U		E
E	N	S	I	G	N		E	N	A	M	O	R

98.

O	D	O	R		A	L	L	A	Y	I	N	G
P		W		S		E		R		M		R
P	A	N	A	C	E	A		O	B	A	M	A
O		E		R		N		M		G		C
R	A	D	I	I		E	V	A	S	I	V	E
T			P		D		T		N		L	
U	P	D	A	T	E		P	H	O	E	B	E
N		E		W		M		E				S
I	N	F	E	R	N	O		R	O	S	E	S
T		L		I		M		A		H		N
I	N	E	R	T		E	X	P	L	O	D	E
E		C		E		N		Y		R		S
S	A	T	U	R	A	T	E		E	E	L	S

99.

P	O	L	I	S	H	E	R		O	S	L	O
A		A		I		L		L		P		X
G	O	I	N	G		I		U	N	I	F	Y
E		D		N		X		G		N		M
			D	I	M	I	N	U	E	N	D	O
E		C		F		R		B		I		R
D	R	O	P	I	N		P	R	O	N	T	O
U		M		C		G		I		G		N
C	O	M	P	A	T	R	I	O	T			
A		O		N		O		U		C		H
T	O	N	I	C		T		S	T	O	V	E
O		L		E		T		L		M		A
R	A	Y	S		P	O	N	Y	T	A	I	L

100.

A	R	C	S		C	A	U	C	U	S	E	S
U		R		S		I		O		U		A
T	R	E	B	L	E	D		U	R	B	A	N
O		D		E		N		U		E		
B	R	O	A	D	C	A	S	T	I	N	G	
A			G		U		E		I		W	
H	I	P		E	I	D	E	R		T	I	E
N		L		H		I		P			L	
	C	A	T	A	S	T	R	O	P	H	I	C
L		C		M			I		Y		O	
I	L	E	U	M		K	I	N	G	D	O	M
M		B		E		I		T		R		E
P	R	O	T	R	U	D	E		R	A	I	D

114

Made in the USA
Coppell, TX
21 August 2021

60965394R00063